Clarinet Secrets

Music Secrets for the Advanced Musician

Music Secrets for the Advanced Musician is designed for instrumentalists, singers, conductors, composers, and other instructors and professionals in music seeking a quick set of pointers to improve their work as performers and creators of music. Easy to use and intended for the advanced musician, contributions to Music Secrets fill a niche for those who have moved far beyond what beginners and intermediate practitioners need. It is the perfect resource for teaching students what they need to know in order to take that next step forward and for reinforcing a set of best practices among advanced and professional musicians.

Clarinet Secrets: 52 Performance Strategies for the Advanced Clarinetist, by Michele Gingras, 2004

Saxophone Secrets: 60 Performance Strategies for the Advanced Saxophonist, by Tracy Lee Heavner, 2013

Oboe Secrets: 75 Performance Strategies for the Advanced Oboist and English Horn Player, by Jacqueline Leclair, 2013

Drum Kit Secrets: 52 Performance Strategies for the Advanced Drummer, by Matt Dean, 2014

Violin Secrets: 101 Strategies for the Advanced Violinist, by Jo Nardolillo, 2015

Voice Secrets: 100 Performance Strategies for the Advanced Singer, by Matthew Hoch and Linda Lister, 2016

Clarinet Secrets: 100 Performance Strategies for the Advanced Clarinetist, Second Edition, by Michele Gingras, 2017

Clarinet Secrets

100 Performance Strategies for the Advanced Clarinetist

Second Edition

Michele Gingras

ROWMAN & LITTLEFIELD
Lanham • Boulder • New York • London

Published by Rowman & Littlefield
A wholly owned subsidary of The Rowman & Littlefield Publishing Group, Inc.
4501 Forbes Boulevard, Suite 200, Lanham, Maryland 20706
www.rowman.com

Unit A, Whitacre Mews, 26-34 Stannary Street, London SE11 4AB

British Library Cataloguing in Publication Information Available

Library of Congress Cataloging-in-Publication Data

Names: Gingras, Michele, 1960–, author.
Title: Clarinet secrets : 100 performance strategies for the advanced clarinetist / Michele
Gingras.
Description: Lanham : Rowman & Littlefield, [2017] | Series: Music secrets for the
advanced musician | Includes bibliographical references and index.
Identifiers: LCCN 2016044323 (print) | LCCN 2016045275 (ebook) | ISBN
9781442276550 (pbk. : alk. paper) | ISBN 9781442276567 (electronic)
Subjects: LCSH: Clarinet—Instruction and study.
Classification: LCC MT380 .G55 2017 (print) | LCC MT380 (ebook) | DDC
788.6/2193—dc23
LC record available at https://lccn.loc.gov/2016044323

♾™ The paper used in this publication meets the minimum requirements of
American National Standard for Information Sciences—Permanence of
Paper for Printed Library Materials, ANSI/NISO Z39.48-1992.

Printed in the United States of America.

To all my students. Thank you for showing
me that one of the best ways
to *learn* about the clarinet is to *teach* the clarinet.

Contents

Preface

This book is written for the advanced clarinetist in need of specific strategies to overcome technical and musical challenges. It is assumed that the reader has already attained a high level of competency on the clarinet and has studied privately with a trusted teacher for a number of years.

Clarinetists love to write about their instrument, and consequently a variety of excellent books already fill our relatively small market. These books describe in detail such topics as embouchure, tone, intonation, tonguing, technique, rhythm, musicianship, repertoire, and reeds. Writers utilize various approaches to explain their ideas. Clarinetists will find that each approach has great value and that one approach may suit them better than another.

Each strategy is explained with accompanying graphics, photos, and musical examples. It is my hope that teachers (clarinetists as well as other wind instrumentalists) will also find the information useful and share it with their students.

In order to tackle each problem immediately, each strategy, or "Secret," is described in a concise manner. Compared to other writings, the order of presentation might seem surprising. Why start off with tonguing in chapter 1, when other relevant issues such as tone and technique are undoubtedly of utmost importance? The answer defines the core of this work.

The advanced clarinetist who is eager to improve right away often hits a wall on challenging techniques such as tonguing, especially rapid tonguing. For this reason, I chose to tackle the very challenging concepts of tonguing in chapter 1. Tone and air management are covered in chapter 2, and chapter 3 discusses intonation, which is often one of the most elusive aspect of clarinetistry. Clarinetists get used to their instrument's tendency to play sharp in the clarion register, therefore losing some sensitivity for accurate pitch.

Chapter 4 discusses many aspects of technique, sight-reading, transposition, and altissimo register; chapter 5 offers ideas on musicianship, memorization, and practice techniques; chapter 6 includes recommendations regarding reeds and equipment; chapter 7 discusses extended techniques and nontraditional repertoire. Each chapter concludes with a smorgasbord of tips on each Quick-Tips Bulletin Board.

The second edition offers new Secrets on tone, technique, transposition, synthetic reeds, and equipment, with improved graphics, musical examples, and photos.

My wish is for this collection of Secrets to read much like the way in which one would approach a box of delicious chocolates. Any Secret can be read in or out of order and chosen depending on one's mood, preference, or need. The topics are many, and the choice is left to the reader to decide which one to "taste" first. In addition, I wanted to vary and enrich my box of chocolates by inviting a select number of guest contributors to bring their own expertise to the table. I consider myself very fortunate to have had the generous and enthusiastic support of several esteemed members of the clarinet profession who provided their knowledge and experience and agreed to be part of the *Secrets* second edition.

The pedagogical ideas gathered in this book are the result of more than thirty years of experience in the clarinet studio and are based on the techniques I believe to have been effective for the majority of my students. Much like a box of chocolates, pedagogy offers a variety of choices and points of view and it is up to the reader to make the selection. Enjoy!

I welcome feedback and comments: gingram@miamioh.edu.

Acknowledgments

The creation of this book was made possible thanks to the support of many people and institutions.

I express special thanks to illustrators Erin Beckloff and Marissa McIntire, photographer Jeff Sabo, as well as Ann Reither and Michael Wilson, who provided invaluable help with graphics and bibliography.

I thank my colleagues who agreed to share their expertise in various Secrets by providing detailed information on some of their specialties: Jean-Luc Blasius (Chalumeau), Dave Camwell (jazz clarinet), John Cipolla (woodwind doubling), Diane Gingras (practice philosophy), Jonathan Gunn (E-flat clarinet), Shelley Jagow (transposition), Doug Monroe (military bands), Greg Oakes (multiphonics), Phillip O. Paglialonga (eliminating cracking in high registers), Ed Palanker (bass clarinet), Robert Spring (super altississimo register), and Simone Weber (German system clarinet).

I also convey my gratitude to my friends and colleagues who provided ideas, inspiration, and editorial advice, and to each and every one of my students who shared their unique talents with me over the years. A most special thanks to Natalie Mandziuk, music acquisitions editor at Rowman & Littlefield.

Finally, I wish to express heartfelt appreciation to Buffet Crampon: Légère Reeds as well as Miami University (Ohio) for its continued support for more than thirty years and Butler University for welcoming me as a new faculty member.

Terminology

The following method is used to describe registers:

| "Low" or "Chalumeau" | "Throat" | "Clarion" | "High" | "Altissimo" |

The following system of notation is used:

Notes below   (middle C): B, A, etc.

Notes immediately above   : d, e, f

"Throat g" will be referred to as "open g," followed by $g^{\#}$, a, and b♭

Clarion notes: b^{1}, c^{1}, etc.

High notes above   : c^{2}, $c^{\#2}$, d^{2}, etc.

Thereafter, notes will be referred to as the altissimo register.

CHAPTER 1

Tonguing Strategies

SECRET 1: ROCKET-SPEED TONGUING

Wouldn't it be splendid if your tongue could bounce effortlessly on and off the reed at rocket speed?

Take a long, well-sharpened wooden pencil and hold it near the eraser between your thumb and index finger. Drop the pencil lead once against a hard surface (keeping your hand a few inches above the surface), and notice how it bounces rapidly after the initial impact. The first impact is the loudest while the following "hits" are rebounds. The fingers are not actually controlling the pencil except for the first motion, much like a stick hitting a snare drum to start a roll.

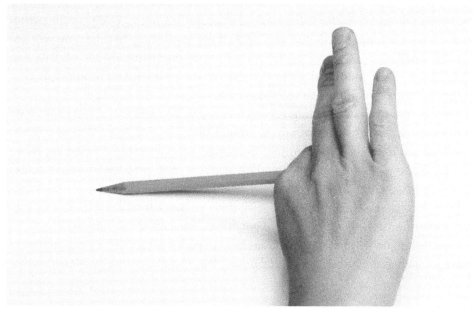

Figure 1.1

Imitate this motion by tonguing repeated notes as follows: Play an open g as two rapid sixteenths; the first note should be accented quite noticeably, while the second should be much softer, echoing the first.

The first note is accented and the repeated note rebounds from the first (think "TA- da," or "TA-la"). Continue by playing three notes (think "TA-da-da," or "TA-la-la"). Follow with four notes: "TA-da-da-da," or "TA-la-la-la." Continue with five, six, then seven notes, and so on. Make sure that the number of notes gradually increases one at a time.

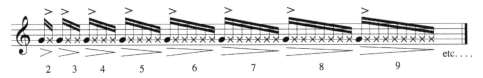

Figure 1.2

After five or six notes, it becomes confusing to count them. Play open g, holding the clarinet with the right hand, and count the notes repeatedly with your left fingers until you have played ten or twelve notes. Remember to accent only the first note, following with effortless soft notes, decreasing the dynamic to virtually nothing.

As you become more agile and comfortable with this exercise, you will notice that the tongue will actually start moving by itself (somewhat uncontrollably), and literally "shake" in a very rapid staccato. Imagine a strong wind blowing through a flag and how the fabric emits a staccato-like noise. Use your air stream to stimulate the tongue to do the very same thing as the flag. In time, you will notice the speed at which your tongue will start to bounce naturally and effortlessly. Carefully monitor your ideal airflow speed and the position and firmness of your tongue for the rapid motion to start happening by itself.

Practice the exercise, playing repeated notes in all registers. Experiment with various dynamics, always strongly accenting the first note more than any other. Continue the exercise by attempting to change notes instead of repeating them, playing basic ascending and descending scales. Later, practice passages across various registers, making sure all notes sound evenly.

If the tongue movements become stiff, think of the soft rebound notes as a rapidly repeating "th" sound, as in the word "thee," instead of "da" or "la."

This technique will be of tremendous help in performing challenging orchestral excerpts such as the *Scherzo* from *A Midsummer Night's Dream* by Mendelssohn.

SECRET 2: ONE-MOTION TONGUING

Playing fast staccato passages can cause fatigue in the tongue muscles, especially if the clarinetist thinks of each tongued note as a single unit. Tonguing in this manner often results in harsh and heavy articulation. On the other hand, if a group of detached notes is regarded as one single motion, most notes in the group become "notes in passing" until the final note is reached, rendering articulation lighter and smoother.

A comparison can be made to a cellist rolling the bow from the lowest to the highest string in one gesture (an arpeggiated chord), rather than stopping the bow between each string. Gliding the bow from one string to the other in a single motion requires relatively little effort, and the result is a smoother sound.

Preparation is necessary before a sound is produced. Initially, the bow is lifted in the air and continues in a circular motion as the strings start to vibrate against the bow. At the end of the gesture, the bow follows through the motion by lifting the arm rather than immediately stopping the arm.

Preparation is also essential when tonguing. As a cellist would lift the bow to begin the gesture, the clarinetist breathes in and exhales through the instrument, starting the first note gently with a light tongue or air attack. Do not focus solely on the first note of a tongued passage; the impetus of the preparation will help launch the excerpt. The first note (and, therefore, the entire grouping) is part of this circular motion and becomes easier to produce.

If we look at the following excerpt of Rossini's *Introduction, Theme and Variations*, Variation 3, we see several groups of seven detached notes. Rather than simply detaching each one, try visualizing each group as a single unit. Start your practice by *slurring* the pattern so all seven notes become one single motion. Then gently tongue all notes, concentrating on the top note only. The in-between notes will naturally sound a little softer, smoother, and more relaxed. Figure 2.1 shows how the tongue starts on No. 1 and aims for No. 2. We can also think of the first and last notes as being *active*, whereas the remaining notes are considered *passive*. The one-motion exercise may also be executed on a descending passage such as the C major arpeggio in the second full bar of Variation 3, or as in Variation 2 of the same work by Rossini.

Adding a crescendo to an ascending or descending passage enhances the overall musical effect and also helps with the tongue's movements. As stated in Secret 1: Rocket-Speed Tonguing, a comparison can be made to wind blowing through a flag. As a strong wind would make the flag vibrate more quickly, thus the tongue could move more rapidly if supported by a strong flow of air throughout staccato passages. Note that, although the airflow is strong, the tongue movements remain very light.

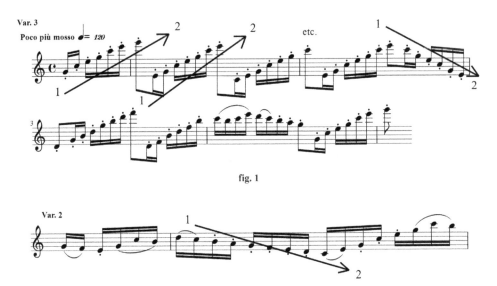

fig. 1

Figure 2.1

SECRET 3: ENERGY-SAVING TONGUING

Often we find that our tongue becomes tired during lengthy staccato sections, mainly because the tongue must execute a number of motions for each single note.

It should be understood that the tongue does not actually touch the reed *during* the short notes. Instead, the sound is released when the tongue is pulled back from the reed, thus allowing the reed to vibrate.

Naturally, the tongue exerts a certain amount of energy for each short note, as if saying "ta-ta." One way to rest the tongue muscles while tonguing is to actually execute some of these staccato notes using the air column rather than the tongue, as if saying "a-ta." For example, a rapid detached scale that would normally be played "TA-ta-ta-ta" could be played "A-ta-ta-ta" instead. (Note that this technique is best used in times of emergency, and that normal rapid tonguing should be practiced diligently.)

Initially, the "a" articulation should be practiced as "ha," using the air column to emulate a staccato sound. If the "ha" attack is played with considerable air speed, it will gradually sound cleaner, resulting in an "a" sound. An excellent orchestral excerpt with which to practice this technique is the *Scherzo* from *A Midsummer Night's Dream* by Mendelssohn. In the excerpt in fig. 3.1, asterisks indicate which notes to play "a" instead of "ta."

Figure 3.1

Since the "a" staccato is played with the air column, it is not practical to use this articulation in the middle of a series of rhythmically equal notes. Rather, this articulation is best used when the rhythm allows for some kind of rest or pause, even as small as a fraction of a second. Therefore, it can be used easily either in the beginning of a passage or when the rhythm shifts.

The *William Tell Overture* by Rossini is also an ideal example for this kind of articulation (see fig. 3.2). Again, asterisks mark where to substitute "a" instead of the usual "ta" articulation.

Figure 3.2

The ♪♫ rhythm is particularly challenging to play rapidly for a long period of time. The "a-ta" technique is ideal for such a passage because one can play "a" instead of "ta" between the eighth note and sixteenth notes for the entire section. With practice, the excerpt can be played at ♩ = 144 with relatively little effort.

Start by practicing the "ha" articulation, increasing the air speed gradually until the airy sound completely disappears from the beginning of each note. Another situation ideally suited for this technique is Reginald Kell's *17 Staccato Studies* (International), *Etude No. 1*. Practice the etude thoroughly with a metronome, increasing the speed gradually. Monitor your progress by writing down each tempo marking after successfully performing an entire section at that speed. For example, when you perform the etude at ♩ = 132, write down the tempo at the top of the page. Do the same when you can play it at ♩ = 138 and so on, until you reach the tempo of ♩ = 170 or faster.

You will be surprised how much faster you can tongue after just a few weeks of mastering this technique.

SECRET 4: FINGER–TONGUE COORDINATION

One of the most challenging aspects of performing rapid staccato passages is the ability to play each note clearly, with perfect tongue and finger coordination. The secret to successfully playing such passages is to master the coordination between the tongue and the fingers.

If the fingers change notes at exactly the same time the tongue executes the staccato, chances are, sooner or later, the passage will become "out of sync" and sound uneven and unclear. Instead, the fingerings should change in anticipation of the tonguing.

As illustrated in fig. 4.1, play low E as short as possible (with both little fingers down), stopping the note with the tongue.

Figure 4.1

As soon as the tongue touches the reed to stop the pitch, quickly lift the left little finger as if you are going to play low F. This F should *not be heard at all*, and the tongue should land on the reed *immediately* after the E is heard. Continuing up the scale, keep the tongue on the reed and repeat the motions, that is, play F as short as possible, stopping the note with the tip of the tongue. As soon as the tongue touches the reed to stop the pitch, quickly lift the right little finger to play G, and so on. During this exercise, the air pressure should remain constant at a fast speed while the tongue is on the reed.

Start slowly, making sure there is a long space between each note to allow adequate preparation for all motions to be executed properly. Avoid the temptation to change fingerings at a slow and comfortable pace. Instead, change the fingering virtually at the same time you are playing the preceding note. The tongue coming back on the reed will silence the next note (think "tat" syllable), and the new fingering will be ready for the next note. Gradually increase the tempo, allowing less and less time between notes.

This exercise is most suitable for short staccato-style passages. Longer articulations do not necessarily require the tongue to return to the tip of the reed. This technique is discussed in Secret 5: Effortless Staccato across All Registers.

Start by playing this exercise in the low register. When a significant level of comfort is reached, advance to the clarion register. Play the exercise in all keys, and continue by varying the exercise, that is, broken thirds, arpeggios, or any combination of notes. Practice short and rapid staccato passages from the clarinet repertoire.

SECRET 5: EFFORTLESS STACCATO ACROSS ALL REGISTERS

Even the most gifted and natural tonguer will agree that rapid articulation can be much more challenging in the upper register compared to the low register. The airflow feels more resistant as soon as the twelfth/register key is used. For this reason, many clarinetists subconsciously increase the air speed in higher registers to compensate and to allow the note to sound more clearly.

If one plays a staccato throat a followed by a staccato b¹ (third line on the staff), the difference in air resistance is very noticeable. There is a "wall" of air resistance starting on b¹ that we seem to want to push through by increasing the airflow. However, increasing the airflow only adds to the problem and creates tension. Clarinetists need to trust that staccato notes in the higher registers will come out effortlessly if they refrain from "crossing the wall" by blowing too forcefully.

A good way to practice this is to play a scale from C to d¹, slurred. Repeat the slurred scale several times until your fingers, body, and air stream are relaxed, and until you have memorized the "feel" of the slurred scale. Play:

Figure 5.1

Continue by playing the same scale (still thinking slurred), and gently tongue each note as if you were still slurring. Make sure the detached scale sounds very similar to the slurred scale, keeping the dynamic quite soft. When playing b¹, noticeably relax the air pressure, and visualize the airflow being directed somewhat downward, as if you were slightly dropping the jaw.

As you gently tongue the ascending C scale, completely relax your body, mindset, tongue, and airflow, and play very softly. Maintain a flat chin embouchure (see Secret 17: Flat Chin exercise), and maintain the best tone possible. Play:

Figure 5.2

If you hear a "bump" or a louder dynamic on b¹ when practicing the detached scale, go back to playing the slurred scale to regain a relaxed airflow. If the bump persists, play the staccato scale without sounding the b¹ and c¹ (play the first six notes detached, continuing to blow air without sound, and tongue through b¹ and

c^1 without letting these notes resonate). Finish the scale with the half-note d^2 sounding normally.

Do the above exercise until you are able to play b^1 and c^1 with the same dynamic and tonal consistency as the other notes.

Practice staccato etudes of intermediate difficulty in this manner, making sure each note above throat b♭ is especially relaxed, blowing and aiming the air slightly downward.

Another way to relax upper register wind resistance is to play a passage with no register key at all. Choose an excerpt that contains notes from the low and clarion registers, and play all the fingerings normally but without adding the register key on the clarion notes. Repeat this exercise until you memorize the "new" melody (without the register key). Next, have a clarinetist friend or colleague sit next to you while you play the passage and have the person press on the register key for you on the appropriate notes (make sure you are still thinking about your new melody with the low notes). You will be amazed at how much easier it will be to tongue the clarion and high registers with these techniques. The greatest challenge will be to retrain the body to relax while tonguing in the high registers without the familiar tension usually associated with tonguing.

SECRET 6: RELAXED JAW

One of the challenges in playing clean, detached notes is to use the tongue without moving the jaw. Indeed, the tongue and jaw muscles naturally tend to work together, but excess jaw movement can affect the intonation and give notes an unstable swooping character because of biting on the reed. Therefore, it is important to be able to dissociate the tongue and jaw movements.

The first task is to relax the jaw so it won't move during tonguing. While looking at yourself in a mirror, gently open your mouth and drop your jaw, as if adopting a "dumbfounded" expression. In this position, see if you can move your tongue in all directions in your mouth. Follow by simply moving the tongue forward and backward, touching the back of the top teeth with the tip of the tongue as if tonguing, but without moving the jaw.

Still keeping the jaw relaxed and dropped, continue the tongue movements, and start saying the syllables "la-la-la" slowly and out loud to see if you can still maintain a relaxed jaw. After you are able to control the "la" syllable, change the syllables to "da-da-da," with the jaw still dropped and motionless. At this point, there should be a conscious feeling of independence between the tongue and jaw muscles. Continue the exercise by slowly saying the syllables "ta-ta-ta," followed by "tat-tat-tat." Closely observe your jaw in the mirror and avoid the slightest jaw movements.

When a greater level of comfort is reached, increase the speed of each syllable until you can tongue very rapidly, still with a motionless jaw.

Test the relaxation level of your jaw muscles by enunciating a few words with the jaw still in the dropped position. First, say phrases that do not require too much lip or jaw movements, such as "I can do this" or "I like to try new things."

Follow with phrases that usually require considerable jaw movements, such as "The best advantage to practicing is obvious." As a ventriloquist would, try finding ways to say the consonants with your tongue instead of the lips and jaw. The result will naturally be less articulate, but understandable nevertheless. The objective is to gain flexibility with the tongue while keeping the jaw motionless, so that when you play short detached notes they will be clear, with a perfectly stable pitch.

After mastering the above exercise, do the very same thing with the mouthpiece and clarinet in playing position, but without actually playing a tone. Continue the exercise by playing open g with the different syllables. Make sure each note's pitch is consistent, without biting the reed or closing the throat, thereby avoiding pitch-swooping effects.

Play detached scales in front of the mirror, increasing the speed gradually. Look very carefully for any jaw movement, and notice how the detached notes get cleaner as you decrease the jaw movements.

When you feel confident that the tongue and jaw muscles can work independently, practice staccato etudes and record them to verify that each note's pitch is stable.

This exercise is helpful for clarinetists who experience tension and pain in the back of the jaw and neck. The elimination of biting also allows the air to flow more freely through the bore, resulting in a cleaner staccato and a fuller tone.

SECRET 7: THE LIGHT TONGUE EXERCISE

Another challenge when playing clean, detached articulation is to achieve full and resonant notes while keeping the tongue movements light and delicate. Because muscles often work together within the body, the tongue naturally tends to crush the reed when the diaphragm projects air in a powerful manner to create a loud dynamic. If the tongue presses too firmly on the tip of the reed, the vibration is hindered when the tongue is removed, resulting in extra noise and response delay before each note is played.

One way to dissociate the contrasting concepts of strong diaphragm action and light tonguing is to teach the tongue to execute light motions during loud dynamics. While playing a *f* long tone on open g, begin moving the tongue *extremely* slowly toward the reed. Gradually allow the tongue to approach the reed in such a microscopic and slow manner that it almost feels like the tongue is pulling away from the tip of the reed instead of moving forward. You might notice that the sound will decrease as your tongue gets closer to the reed. This is caused by the tendency of the tongue and the diaphragm to move with equal strength when working together. As you allow the tongue to slowly approach the reed, remember to keep the dynamic full and strong. As soon as the tip of the tongue finally touches the reed, remove it *immediately*. Repeat this until you achieve control of the tongue, and remember to free the jaw of any tension. The result should sound similar to the syllables "lah, lah, lah."

The second step of this exercise consists of keeping the tongue on the reed instead of removing it quickly. Play a long open g loudly, then approach the reed with the tip of the tongue slowly, and gently leave it on the tip of the reed (stopping the sound) for a few seconds *while continuing to blow*. Release the tongue to create a clear, resonant, and full note, and repeat the motions. The result should sound similar to the syllables "dat-dat-dat."

To practice short staccato, play a long open g loudly, touch the reed gently with the tongue (stopping the sound), and remove it very quickly only to put it back on the reed immediately and repeatedly, making sure the air pressure remains constant. The result should sound similar to the syllables "tat-tat-tat."

As the illustrations in fig. 7.1 demonstrate, it is important to touch the reed with as little tongue surface as possible so the airflow can resume immediately when the tongue is removed.

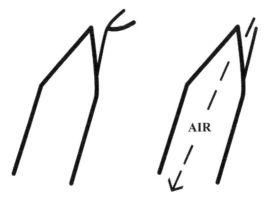

The tip of the tongue touches the reed extremely lightly, allowing the reed to vibrate immediately after the tongue is released.

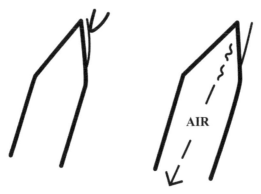

Too much tongue touches and crushes the reed, delaying the immediate reed response after the tongue is released.

Figure 7.1

SECRET 8: PING!

The clarinet tone has the capacity of being so resonant that one can almost feel the wood vibrating, especially when playing accents. The key to playing ringing accents and articulations is to make each note sound as bouncy as possible, as if the notes were exploding out of the instrument, resulting in a "ping" syllable.

If the note to be articulated is not readily "manufactured" in the mind and body, the note will have less ring, and the beginning of the note will be unclear.

The idea is to build the note *before* it is sounded. Prepare the note with your mind, ears, embouchure, tongue, diaphragm, and airflow, as if manufacturing the entire "product" before allowing it out in public.

Before starting an accented note, gently place the tip of the tongue on the tip of the reed. Start building the air pressure by blowing while maintaining the tongue position on the reed. When you feel that the air pressure is strong enough to result in a full, resonant note, release the tongue quickly, making absolutely sure that the air pressure is not diminished at all (it should actually *increase*) before you remove the tongue. Repeat this exercise until you hear a clear and extremely resonant "ping!" at the beginning of each note.

An ideal note with which to initiate this exercise is c^1. Take your time to build the air pressure sufficiently so that each attack "pings":

"Ping!" "Ping!"

Figure 8.1

After achieving clear accents and mastering note attacks, it is also important to control note endings. As presented later in Secret 26: Dissecting Tone, note attacks and decays vary in style depending on the musical characteristics of a passage, as illustrated in fig. 8.2.

When a note is very short, both the attack and the decay are brief and clear. The "ping" appears in the beginning of each short attack, and it is interrupted by a sudden stop in the sound to allow the next note to start immediately thereafter. In contrast, an accented note also begins with a "ping" attack but ends with a slow decay because the air column is being used instead of the tongue to stop the sound.

It is important to remember that even though each note is very short during rapid staccato, there is still enough time to begin each attack with a healthy "ping." The sound is continuous, the air moves steadily forward, and the tongue simply

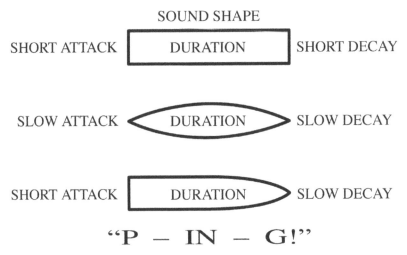

Figure 8.2

interrupts the rapid airflow. Avoid biting on the reed so note endings will not change shape or be pinched. Visualize the diagram in fig. 8.3.

Try various octaves and articulation lengths so each register resonates evenly throughout the entire range.

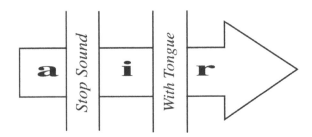

Figure 8.3

SECRET 9: ARTICULATION VOCABULARY

Advanced clarinetists should master a wide variety of articulation combinations. In order to become a consistent and reliable player, it is important to remember some basic rules so articulations will remain consistent from one phrase to another. These rules are as follows:

1. Lean on the first note of a slur
2. Decrescendo slightly on each slur
3. Clip the last note of a slur if followed by a staccato

Naturally, these rules may be somewhat flexible, depending on the style of music performed, as well as personal choice. For example, articulations can be interpreted with all kinds of syllables, such as "la," "da," "dat," "ta," "tat," "tah," and so on.

The idea is to build a basic articulation "palette" that will become consistent, predictable, and reliable. A lack of consistency may result in unclear musical phrasing, not to mention misunderstandings while rehearsing with other musicians.

It is important not to breathe between two very short notes. For example, when playing example 2 on the next page, "TA-a-yat-tat," the syllables "yat-tat" are joined together with a tongue movement, with no breath between the two notes. Try this exercise: First, play a repeated chromatic scale slurred, from e to e¹ and back down:

Repeat several times

Figure 9.1

Play the same scale with each of the articulation combinations listed in fig. 9.2. If all three articulation rules are followed carefully, you will notice how vastly different the articulation patterns will sound, as if each pattern has its own "sound personality." I encourage you to practice each one diligently and increase the speed gradually.

Articulation (play)	Syllables (think)
 1	"**TA**-a-a-a-**TA**-a-a-a"
 2	"**TA**-a-yat-tat-**TA**-a-yat-tat"
 3	"**TA**-yat-tat-tat-**TA**-yat-tat-tat"
 4	"tat-**TA**-a-at-tat-**TA**-a-at"
 5	"tat-**TA**-a-**TA**-a-**TA**-a-**TA**"
 6	"tat-**TA**-yat-tat-tat-**TA**-yat-tat"
 7	"**TA**-a-**TA**-a-**TA**-a-**TA**-a"
 8	"**TA**-a-a-**TA**-a-a-**TA**-a-a . . ."
 9	"(a)-**TA**-a-a-a-**TA**-a-a-a . . ."
 10	"tat-tat-**TA**-yat-tat-tat-**TA**-yat"
 11	"**TA**-yat-tat-tat-tat-tat-tat-tat"
 12	"tat-tat-tat-tat-tat-tat-tat-tat"

Figure 9.2

SECRET 10: DOUBLE TONGUING

Although it is a fantastic technical tool, double tonguing rarely can match the clarity of single tonguing. With practice, one can acquire a fast single tongue and it should indeed be used most of the time. On the other hand, clarinet articulation tends be more difficult than flute or trumpet. Playing double staccato can produce a great effect and matches well with other instruments that use the technique. Clarinet double tonguing requires less effort in the lower register because the air resistance is not as strong compared to the high register. For this reason, double tonguing practice should start in the low register.

Play a low G, alternating the syllables "ta" and "ka," or "teh" and "keh." Play long syllables at first to stabilize the sound as much as possible. As when speaking, play "ta" with the tip of the tongue and "ka" with the back of the tongue. Attack the "ta" note normally, then change lightly to "ka," making sure the airflow stays even. Initially, the "ka" tongue movement may result in a distorted tone, but diligent practice and minimal tongue movement will eventually remedy the problem.

When both notes match in quality, increase the tempo. If you are squeaking when playing "ka," your tongue is moving too much and distorting the airflow. An excellent alternative is "ga" or "gi" (as in "gig"). The syllable "gi" has the advantage of allowing the embouchure to remain somewhat closed and motionless. Similarly, the "ta" and "teh" syllables can be substituted with "da" and "dee."

One way to improve double tonguing is to practice saying different syllables while *not* playing. While taking a walk or driving, for example, practice saying the syllables "ta-ga-da" (stop), "ta-ga-da" (stop) as fast as possible between the stops. Continue by adding two syllables each time. Say: "ta-ga-da-ga-da" (stop), and repeat. Add two more syllables: "ta-ga-da-ga-da-ga-da" (stop), and so on. The first spoken syllable should be accented, and the remaining syllables should be smooth, quick, and soft. In time, these vocal exercises should facilitate double tonguing on the clarinet.

Another way to think of the "ga" syllable is to actually include it at the end of the "ta" syllable, as in the word "tag." The result is "tag-gad-dag-gad-dag," allowing each release to tie into the next attack. This minimizes tongue motion and increases the tongue's speed.

After you've improved your tongue dexterity, try to play slow and fast scales to synchronize your fingers with the double tonguing movements. Play scales (or sections of scales) in the low register on a daily basis, and start adding a note or two each day until you can play two- and three-octave scales. An ideal orchestral excerpt to practice at this stage is the *second* clarinet part of the *Scherzo* from *A Midsummer Night's Dream* by Mendelssohn.

The secret to double tonguing is *patience*, as this particular technique usually takes quite some time to master. Double tonguing with a double lip embouchure can help during initial practice.

Double tonguing technique is an invaluable tool in contemporary music, and it is very useful in difficult and extremely fast orchestral excerpts, such as the rapid sixteenth-note passages in Beethoven's Fourth Symphony. Seasoned double tonguers can have a ball playing violin repertoire arrangements such as *Hora Staccato* by Grigoras Dinicu.

SECRET 11: FLUTTER TONGUING

Flutter tonguing is a technique involving rolling the tongue near the reed to produce a "Rrrrr" sound. The effect is mostly used in contemporary music, such as
in Alban Berg's *Vier Stücke* op. 5 for clarinet and piano. It is also a common
technique in jazz. Flutter tonguing is somewhat more challenging for clarinetists
compared to flute or trumpet because the mouthpiece is in the way of the tongue.

Also called *Flatterzunge* (German), the technique involves quickly rolling the
tip of the tongue against the roof of the mouth (like a Spanish "r") while playing,
without touching the reed with the tongue.

For better results, start a note with the syllable "harr," rather than "tarr." Starting with an "h" attack prevents the tongue from touching the reed, which would
cause the sound to stop. Increasing the air speed and relaxing the tongue allow the
tongue to roll freely and effectively. A comparison can be made with a flag flut-
tering in the wind. If the flag is light and flexible, it will flutter freely, as opposed
to a stiff flag that would not flutter as well. Flutter tonguing is most challenging in
soft dynamics and high registers. Consciously relax the tongue muscles and blow
air constantly and keep the air moving to imitate the flag principle.

For individuals who cannot roll their tongue for various reasons, there are two
substitute techniques. One involves playing the written note while singing a pitch
that is dissonant to the written note, and the other is rolling the back of the throat
and tongue (as in French or German dry "r" pronunciation).

See the musical examples in fig. 11.1 for various notations for flutter tongue.
The abbreviations are f.t. (English) or *flz* (German) and *ord.* ("ordinary" for normal tone).

Figure 11.1

SECRET 12: SLAP TONGUING

Slap tongue is a fun popping or percussive sound used mostly in jazz and avant-garde, as well as some folk music. The way you choose to play slap tongue depends on which technique feels natural or easiest for you. As you gain experience, you will find the one that sounds the loudest and most effective. There are three ways to slap tongue:

Spitting Motion

Practice a spitting motion without your instrument. Then lay your tongue flat on the majority of the reed's surface and push it against the reed. While the tongue is pushing the reed shut, compress the air in your mouth, and suddenly release the tongue and airflow while dropping the jaw. Stop blowing soon after so that the slap tongue will sound without pitch. The tongue starts on the reed and ends off the reed.

Suction Motion

Practice loudly clapping or snapping your tongue away from the palate (much like kids do) without your instrument. Practice the same technique with the index finger in the mouth instead of your instrument. Lay your tongue flat on a large portion of the finger and "unglue" or remove it quickly by releasing your air and dropping your jaw, and make a slapping or "clack" noise. Next, using your instrument, lay your tongue flat on the majority of the reed's surface. Imagine your tongue is glued to the reed, create a suction, and quickly slap it away from the reed while you blow. Stop blowing soon after so that the slap tongue "note" will sound without pitch. The tongue starts on the reed and ends off the reed.

Popping Motion

Practice loudly popping your pursed lips (much like kids do) without your instrument. Squeeze the reed shut with the lips while compressing the air in the mouth and then, suddenly release the compressed air through the reed and mouthpiece, ending with your tongue on the reed. Unlike the two previous techniques, the tongue starts *off* the reed and ends *on* the reed. The slap tongue is the result of the air pressure suddenly entering the clarinet bore, only to be stopped immediately by the tongue.

All of the movements described above should be done very quickly. It is helpful to start practicing slap tongue with a soft reed for short periods of time, as the technique can be tiring for the tongue muscles. Also, extended practice can damage reeds, so use old reeds or synthetic reeds that are more resilient.

All of the above techniques can either sound very short with no pitch or be combined with a tone if you blow longer after the slap tongue is played. The larger the instrument, the louder the sound, so slap tongue can sound spectacular on bass clarinet, especially in the low register. Practice all kinds of scale patterns, and experiment with rhythms interspersed with random rests or air noises to create stunning effects. Examples of notations for slap tongue are shown in fig. 12.1.

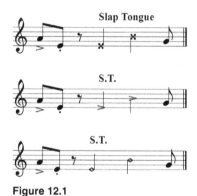

Figure 12.1

CHAPTER 2

Intonation Strategies

SECRET 13: PRACTICING WITH THE DRONE

Clarinets are designed to be slightly sharp so the tuning barrel can be pulled out more or less as needed. It is common to pull out the barrel after warming up because warmer air causes the pitch to rise. Even if the barrel is positioned properly, clarinetists tend to play sharp because of biting on the reed when playing in the clarion and high registers. Clarinetists often find that biting on the reed is quite comfortable because doing so initially seems to provide a sense of stability with the embouchure and requires less air support. Unfortunately, not only does the pitch rise but also the tone becomes thin and devoid of harmonics or partials.

To enrich the sound, it is imperative to recognize the value of precise intonation. Our fellow string players constantly address this issue by hearing *intervals* rather than concentrating solely on individual pitches. Without this approach, violinists would find it impossible to play in tune. However, clarinetists often rely on set fingerings and customarily do not pay close attention to intonation in the early years of training. Hearing the distance between two notes instead of tuning one sustained note will prove a most efficient way to understand and master accurate intonation.

Another important consideration is that acoustic characteristics of our instrument cause some notes to be flat or sharp, and this can negatively affect our perception of correct pitch. For example, octaves are sometimes sharp (the distance between the two notes is too wide) because the register tube is designed to accommodate two functions: To play the clarion notes *and* to play the throat b♭. Therefore, the register tube's width has to be drilled wide enough to produce an acceptable b♭, yet narrow enough so the clarion notes won't sound sharp. Unfortunately, a perfect compromise is yet to be designed, as the register tube is still too wide for the clarion register. At the same time, however, the register tube is too small, which explains the b♭ infamous "airy" quality. Clarinetists who tend to bite on the reed develop a "sharp" ear and end up not noticing sharp notes, and consequently they do not always lower the pitch when necessary.

Practice measuring intervals by playing long tones with a tuner equipped with a "sound feature" or a tuner app so a drone can be played with the long tones simultaneously. After warming up and tuning to A = 440 Hz, start playing a C major scale *very slowly* against a concert b♭ drone (tonic). Notice the different intervals being created with each changing note (in clarinet pitch): Unison (c-c), major second (c-d), major third (c-e), and so on. Tune each interval carefully, and memorize the pitch tendencies of your instrument. Play two octaves (slurred) up and down, and measure each interval against the drone. After doing this exercise on the C scale for about thirty minutes, turn off the drone and play the same slow scale without the drone. If the exercise is done patiently and correctly, something incredible will start to happen. You will begin to actually hear the two-note intervals you heard earlier, even though the drone is now absent. The C drone will be so anchored in your memory that you will mentally hear it as you play the scale. Do the same exercise with various scales, and choose notes other than the tonic as the drone. Play scales against the drone's third or fifth.

After studying your instrument's intonation tendencies and correcting sharp notes without biting, you will notice your tone becoming deeper and richer. Continue this technique by practicing your repertoire using the drone during the entire practice session. Play a piece along with a variety of drone notes, especially the passages where you find your pitch to be inconsistent. Write these inconsistencies on your music until you are able to predict which notes will need adjustment.

The clarinet also has a tendency to be sharp in soft dynamics, especially during decrescendos. Stare at the tuner needle and see if you can decay a note without raising its pitch at the end.

Another problem with the clarinet is that, invariably, initial attacks are sharp. Correct this by "under-attacking" problematic notes. Lower the jaw slightly before starting a note and notice how you will be right on target (instead of being sharp) and remain in tune for the duration of the note. I urge clarinetists to use the drone technique as often as necessary and throughout their entire careers. The satisfaction of accurate intonation is immeasurable.

SECRET 14: HEARING DIFFERENCE TONES

The drone exercise in Secret 13 describes ways to practice with a drone to greatly improve intonation skills. As your ear becomes more discerning, you will start hearing the occurrence of "difference tones" while playing specific notes against the drone.

A difference tone (or "combination tone," or "resultant tone") is an additional pitch that is produced when two individual tones are played simultaneously. The resulting distortion from the two pitches creates a third, less audible tone. With a well-trained ear, the player will not only hear this new tone, but will also be able to identify its pitch and modify it with the embouchure.

Sometimes, depending on which notes are played, no difference tones appear (see quarter rest below, second line, third bar). However, other intervals naturally cause difference tones to occur. As the following example illustrates, a drone on concert f♯¹ played against a clarion b¹ on B♭ clarinet creates e; the same f♯ against the clarinet's c¹ creates A♯, and so on. By slightly modifying the embouchure, each difference tone's pitch can be manipulated up or down, thus changing the intonation or frequency of the tone. Practicing this way enhances listening skills and intonation precision.

Figure 14.1

SECRET 15: TUNING WITH THE PIANO

Tuning with the piano offers interesting challenges for the clarinetist. The piano cannot vary in pitch to accommodate changing melodic or harmonic contexts because the strings (with even-tempered intonation) are simply struck by the keyboard hammers and intonation cannot be adjusted. In contrast, the pitch of the clarinet can be varied at will and is, therefore, more flexible when subtle pitch adjustments are required. Clarinetists who perform with piano accompaniment must find a compromise to play in tune with a less flexible instrument. Some notes on the clarinet will have a natural pitch tendency (either flat or sharp). If these tendencies are not addressed in rehearsal, the pitches will not be adjustable until rests in the music allow sufficient time to position the barrel accordingly.

For example, b² in the clarion register will tend to be sharp, whereas e will tend to be flat. A compromise must be reached between the two notes. As the following example illustrates, I suggest tuning b¹, open g, e, and b² consecutively while the piano is playing concert a. A flat e is a strong indicator that you will be flat throughout the performance, and a sharp b² indicates that you will be sharp in general. Pull out the barrel until b² is correct; however, if the e becomes flat, compromise by immediately pushing in the barrel slightly, and lower the b² with your jaw instead. A sharp note can always be lowered with the embouchure during a performance, but a flat note will generally remain flat unless the barrel is pushed in.

Figure 15.1

Resonating Piano Strings

Another technique to tune with the piano is to play a note with the clarinet bell pointing toward the piano strings while the pianist simply presses on the sustain pedal *without playing a single note.* Play a sustained note on the clarinet and hear how the piano strings react to this note. If you hear "beats" or a shaking pitch, this means you are not in tune with the piano (several piano strings are vibrating). If, on the contrary, only one piano string vibrates beautifully without any distortion for several seconds (on the same pitch as the clarinet), it means your pitch is perfect.

SECRET 16: USING FINGERS TO MODIFY INTONATION

Intonation can be tricky for clarinetists. So many factors come into play when adjusting pitch, such as temperature, embouchure, and instrument design. Fortunately, the clarinet is equipped with rings instead of pads covering tone holes, so one can learn to easily manipulate the intonation by effectively adjusting the size of each hole, even on the most stubborn notes.

For example, the throat tones tend to lack resonance and be sharp. To improve tone color and intonation, most advanced clarinetists cover additional tone holes when playing throat tones. The exact fingerings can vary, depending on the instrument and embouchure.

Because basic fingerings for the throat notes involve so few closed tone holes, the result is an extremely short resonance tube. Closing additional tone holes helps lengthen the tube, which in turn darkens the sound. My suggestion is to experiment with various fingerings to see which ones work best with your instrument. For example, covering the left and right middle and ring fingers will lengthen the tube (leave the index fingers open), resulting in clear resonance rather than a fuzzy tone quality. Adding the F/c^1 key is another option. Experiment, but begin playing the corresponding resonance fingerings for each note shown in figure 16.1. To lower the pitch of low A, place the right ring finger partially over the low G tone hole to interrupt the airflow (fig. 16.2).

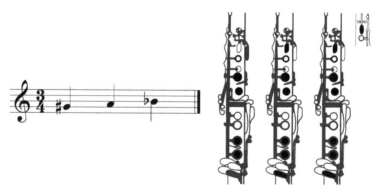

Figure 16.1

Figure 16.2

Pivoting your finger up or down depending on the desired pitch correction, bending the airflow rather than blocking it; this way the pitch is lowered and the sound quality is not jeopardized (fig. 16.3).

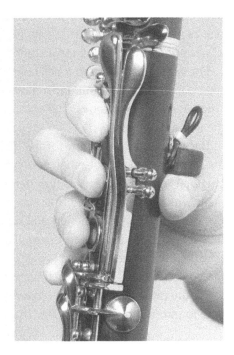

Figure 16.3

To lower the pitch of low B, place the right ring finger partially over the low G tone hole in the same manner as stated above. Or, for the "forked" low B, place the middle *joint* of the right middle finger *almost* completely over the B tone hole (fig. 16.4).

B fingering   **forked B fingering**

Figure 16.4

To lower the pitch of throat f♯, add the left ring finger. Be careful not to blow too much; this will distort the tone. Play what is shown in fig. 16.5.

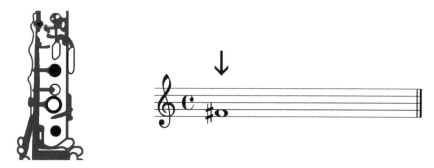

Figure 16.5

There are numerous ways to vary the above examples. Use acoustic logic and listen carefully when choosing fingerings.

SECRET 17: FLAT CHIN

Embouchure is crucial to producing a good tone. Generally, clarinet students are taught to flatten the chin and wrap the lips around the mouthpiece in an "o" shape.

While most muscles are easily controlled (such as fingers, cheeks, and tongue), the chin muscles are more difficult to move independently. Before being able to move the chin muscles with ease and precision, one must be aware of how these muscles work.

Try this exercise: while keeping your jaw firmly closed, try moving the chin muscles up and down. The upward motion is naturally easier. Concentrate on stretching the chin's skin and muscles as much as possible *without* moving the closed jaw. This exercise should be done until control of the chin muscles is easily achieved (see fig. 17.1).

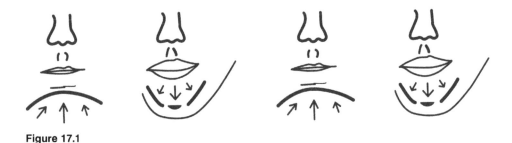

Figure 17.1

The reason for stretching the chin muscles is that the reed needs to vibrate against a firm surface, that is, the lower lip and teeth, so the reed vibrations will not be hindered or exaggerated. A soft chin embouchure allows the lower lip to become too loose and makes the reed vibrate uncontrollably, resulting in a flat and colorless tone. The chin might also be touching the reed, therefore dampening the sound. The upper teeth should rest near the tip of the mouthpiece (see fig. 17.2).

The chin is stretched (correct)   The chin is relaxed (incorrect)

Figure 17.2

Example A below illustrates a proper angle. The lower lip should lie near where the curve between the mouthpiece and the reed starts. This avoids squeezing the reed against the mouthpiece, causing the sound to choke (see example B). A helpful hint is to gently push the right thumb (under the thumb rest) toward the upper teeth in order to avoid the tendency to bite while playing in the upper registers.

A good and effective clarinet embouchure permits control of the most subtle color changes in the sound. A correct distribution of lip, jaw, and chin tightness (50 percent upward, 50 percent downward) is illustrated in example C of fig. 17.3.

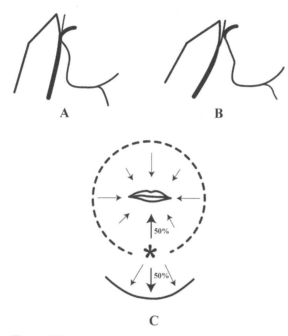

Figure 17.3

As the lips follow the contour of the mouthpiece to prevent air leaks and to equalize the embouchure, the chin is stretched downward. Note the opposition of pressure at the * sign; the resulting tension is the key to a resonating tone. The goal is to find an ideal middle ground where the chin's tension is divided equally. Diligent practice should determine the best distribution of pressure on the reed for each individual. Biting too much narrows the tone and gives it a buzzy quality, while relaxing too much takes the center of the tone away and adds an air noise to the sound. Emulating the flat chin as if shaving or drinking out of a narrow straw are creative ways of achieving the flat chin position.

SECRET 18: THREE-STEP EMBOUCHURE

Secret 17's chin exercise describes the importance of a flat chin embouchure to achieve a centered and resonant tone.

Here, I would like to address how to maximize tone by practicing the three-step embouchure. Students often form their embouchures in two steps: take in the mouthpiece and seal the lips around it. Adding a third step of *taking in more reed* before forming a seal around the mouthpiece allows more reed surface to vibrate, resulting in a bigger and darker tone. Here are the three steps:

1. Place the top teeth near the tip of the mouthpiece.
2. Without moving the top teeth down the mouthpiece, slide the lower lip and jaw down the reed to the point at which the reed meets the mouthpiece rails.
3. Bring the lips' corners inward in an "O" shape, flatten the chin, and blow. Note that step number two is particularly important because taking in more reed prevents biting and sharpness. The result is a more resonant tone and more accurate intonation.

STEP 1   STEP 2   STEP 3

Figure 18.1

SECRET 19: TRAINING WHEEL FOR LOWERING THE PITCH

Intonation is an extremely important aspect of achieving a beautiful tone. Young clarinetists will often have problems with the pitch being flat because of the developmental stage of their embouchure. However, advanced clarinetists often have a tendency to play sharp because of biting the reed. Intonation problems can also be caused by acoustic properties of the instrument as well as several other factors.

Nevertheless, students who play with extremely sharp intonation for several years will end up "tuning" their ears to a higher pitch and will have great difficulty in hearing correct intonation. A sharp tone usually sounds quite small and metallic, as most harmonics are cut off by the biting jaw.

To help clarinetists adjust their ears to a flatter pitch, I suggest installing a "training wheel" in the instrument for a few weeks. Simply cut a one-and-three-quarter-inch (46 mm) or slightly shorter piece of half-inch-wide (13 mm) waterproof first-aid tape, and insert it in the bore at the top part of the upper joint, as illustrated below. Make sure the tape is affixed flat on the bore's surface.

Figure 19.1

The principle of this technique is similar to sticking smaller pieces of tape in tone holes to lower the pitch. Interestingly, the tape seems to lower the crucial notes and leave other notes intact. While throat tones do not seem to be affected by the tape, the clarion notes, which are usually sharp, sound flatter. It is important, however, to make sure to add just one piece of tape. Adding too much tape results in highly uneven pitch and a muffled sound. Note that these calculations are made on the basis of A = 440 Hz as the standard pitch. Different tape lengths, embouchure techniques, and barrel specifications affect the pitch substantially.

Having this tape inside the bore should be considered a temporary solution to allow the player to continually hear a lower pitch, which in turn will deepen and enrich the sound. When the tape is removed, the performer will simply not accept sharp pitch or thin tone quality anymore and will become more sensitive to correct intonation.

Choose a waterproof first-aid tape to avoid water accumulation. You might find that water still accumulates on the surface of the tape and that the register tube needs frequent drying. Warming the top joint under your arm before practicing can help reduce the amount of water condensation.

The tape might be removed inadvertently while swabbing the instrument. To prevent this problem, insert the tape while the bore is *dry,* and refrain from drying the top part of the bore once it becomes humid following the first practice session. The next practice day, swab the top joint with a small silk swab to prevent the tape from coming off. The tape should become adhered to the surface quite firmly after a few days. If not, insert a recorder brush through the bottom of the joint and use the silk swab with the tip of a finger to pat dry the top section without pulling the tape off.

After a few weeks of practicing the drone exercise (see Secret 13: Practicing with the Drone), either remove the tape, or gradually reduce its length until correct intonation is comfortably achieved without the tape.

SECRET 20: TUNING GAMES

Once you become more advanced as an instrumentalist and develop your ability to recognize subtle variations in pitch, you can perfect your intonation skills by playing some tuning games.

Game 1: Playing Flatter Than A = 440 Hz

Play a memorized line while looking at the tuner needle (on a tuner or a tuner app) to make sure you are in tune at A = 440 Hz, then calibrate your tuner one notch lower at A = 439 Hz and play the same line with the lower pitches. At first, this may be extremely difficult and your tone may suffer in quality; however, your ear will signal your jaw to open, which will eventually result in a more resonant tone and lower pitch.

After playing with the tuner needle at A = 439 Hz successfully, test yourself again, this time using the drone. After a few days of repositioning your jaw to play at A = 439 Hz, do the same exercises one notch lower, with the calibration set at A = 438 Hz.

Ask a friend to practice the same exercises independently and, after a few days, get together and practice a musical line in unison. Try to keep the line in tune together at both calibrations as consistently as possible. Play the line first at A = 439 Hz, and then try the same line in unison at A = 438 Hz.

Once you resume practicing on your own with the tuner at A = 440 Hz, you will notice how much easier it is to control your intonation and to play in tune, as well as how rich and resonant your tone has become.

Game 2: Intonation Competition

With the same friend, test your intonation ability by asking your practice partner to play a musical line purposefully out of tune and try to match the pitches as closely as possible. Ask your practice partner to play notes randomly out of tune (some flat, some sharp), as well as notes that are in tune. Bite on the reed to sharpen notes and lower the jaw to play flatter. After playing the line a few times, switch roles. Biting on the reed will only be done for this game and should be avoided in performance. The intonation competition game will undoubtedly result in some good laughs but is a challenging tuning exercise, nonetheless.

Another helpful and fun way to practice with a tuner is to use the SmartMusic virtual accompaniment software, available through an online subscription. It visually shows how to adjust the pitch, and it can play a simultaneous reference note while tuning. The drone feature is helpful to learn how to tune intervals. A computer microphone is necessary to make use of these tools. Visit smartmusic.com.

Being proficient at intonation means that you can be flexible in all kinds of situations, including playing in tune with "out of tune" players. Your confidence as a performer will increase and you will be pleased to notice the improvement in your intonation control in chamber music and ensemble settings.

SECRET 21: PLAYING WITH A VERY SOFT REED TO ELIMINATE BITING

Biting on the reed is a common problem with the clarinet embouchure. It may seem natural to bite on the reed; however, doing so results in a small tone and sharp intonation. A thin tone does not project well and contains very few harmonics, making it less rich and less resonant.

One way to help to eliminate biting is to practice with a very soft reed (#1.5 or #2 strength). The first time you try to play with the soft reed, you may inadvertently squeeze the reed shut and prevent it from producing a sound. This will be the first indication that, indeed, you have a tendency to bite.

After practicing with the soft reed for a few days, you will be able to play almost anything without choking it against the tip of the mouthpiece. Naturally, your tone will be far from ideal, sounding buzzy, reedy, thin, and unappealing. Luckily, there is a light at the end of the tunnel. You will learn to keep your jaw open, allowing the reed to vibrate freely. Also, your airflow will increase, adding substance to your tone and improving your intonation.

Practice with the soft reed in a private location and unveil your success once you have achieved an embouchure that produces a rich tone. Use a tuner to make sure you play consistently at A = 440 Hz and keep your airflow at a maximum. Since your jaw will now be more open, there will be more room for the air to flow, resulting in a bigger tone and more accurate pitch.

It is best to use the soft reed for only a few minutes each day, as it is a little unpleasant for the ears. It will be worth the effort and sooner rather than later you will get used to your new embouchure and play with a more professional tone once you go back to your regular reeds.

SECRET 22: EAR TRAINING FOR CLARINETISTS

One problem faced by young clarinetists is pitch identification. Indeed, when a band director asks the group to tune to a B♭, clarinetists first need to transpose the note mentally in order to play the same pitch as the other instruments. In this case, clarinetists play a C fingering to match the B♭ concert pitch and internalize or see another note name, negatively affecting their note recognition skills.

Clarinetists face another interesting challenge. Since the clarinet key system is very well designed for fast technique, gifted players often become "technical wizards" in a relatively short period of time. Compared to violinists or horn players who must "hear" each pitch before playing it accurately, clarinetists can get away with simply executing correct fingerings to play technical passages reasonably well in tune. Although this offers many advantages, it can diminish clarinetists' ability to accurately hear pitch while playing.

Clarinetists who study ear training early on will immediately see an improvement in their technique because they can "hear" the notes before playing them. The combination of recognizing fingerings with the written notes along with pitch recognition will enable the player to react more quickly. Additionally, clarinetists who are acutely aware of pitch can refine their intonation skills significantly.

Another bonus for clarinetists who study ear training is that they will be better prepared should they wish to major in music in college. Clarinetists who study ear training have better chances of improving their results in ear training and sight-singing placement tests administered on the day of their audition.

Aside from taking ear-training classes in school or with a tutor, some easy-to-use and fun websites such as musictheory.net offer extremely helpful practice tools to improve an array of music theory topics and even include a staff paper generator.

To be successful musicians, we need to make the most of our abilities. A well-trained ear is a valuable asset for improvement of intonation and technique. The tools for ear training are more readily available than ever, and the sooner we get started, the sooner we will realize the benefits.

QUICK-TIPS BULLETIN BOARD—INTONATION

- To keep intonation consistent, start with the tuning barrel pushed all the way in and wait until your instrument is warmed up before pulling it out gradually. After playing a few minutes, the intonation will rise along with the instrument's bore temperature. Check with your tuner and pull out the barrel accordingly.
- Avoid biting on the reed. If necessary, practice with a double-lip embouchure for a few minutes every day, at least until you master a free-blowing embouchure.
- Avoid smothering your clarinet between your knees when you play while seated. This hinders the tone of low notes and affects the intonation. Additionally, this may contribute to increased tension in the body.
- What part of the instrument should you pull when your instrument is sharp? In general, pull out the barrel to flatten the left-hand and throat notes. Pull out between the two middle joints to flatten the right-hand notes, and the bell to flatten the low E and middle b^1.
- When you end a note, do not end it by biting on the reed. Instead, keep your airflow steady and use the diaphragm to end the note.
- Because basic fingerings for the throat notes involve so few closed tone holes, the resonance tube is extremely short. Closing additional tone holes helps lengthen the tube, which in turn darkens the sound and lowers intonation. My suggestion is to experiment with many fingerings to see which ones work best with your instrument.
- Intonation can be adjusted by partly closing some tone holes with various fingers. Use acoustic logic and listen carefully when choosing fingerings.

CHAPTER 3

Tone Strategies

SECRET 23: BREATHING

Acoustic musical instruments need a resonance chamber to produce a full tone. The most significant part of the body of a string instrument is the resonance box. Singers use their bodies as resonance chambers, and virtually all percussion and keyboard instruments are constructed with resonance boxes of some kind.

On the other hand, high wind and brass instruments have relatively small chambers of resonance. Thankfully, a wind instrument's bore is designed to allow the sound to be naturally amplified. I like to take this idea further by suggesting you use your body as a resonance chamber to enhance the instrument's sound capacity. Obviously, if the lungs (resonance box) are filled with air before playing a note, the tone will sound much richer than if a note is started with empty lungs.

Develop the good habit of fully and consistently expanding the lungs and breathing fully before playing a phrase. Not only will this increase the sound's resonance, but it will allow the phrase to begin with more intent, resulting in a smoother and clearer start, whether it be legato or detached.

This technique can be demonstrated by attempting to speak loudly with empty lungs and air-filled lungs. Clearly, the voice will have much more depth and carrying power if the body's resonance cage is expanded and open. To ensure maximum resonance, a proper breathing technique is required both for inhalation and exhalation.

Inhaling

First, the body needs to be correctly positioned in order to allow the lungs to fully expand when inhaling. Stand up with a straight back, feeling each vertebra separating from the others. Pull your shoulders back slightly, and relax your abdomen and arms. You are now ready to inhale.

Since a full sound requires adequate airflow, taking in a lot of air is important. To allow the air to enter freely into the lungs, open your throat as if yawning. While inhaling, you should be hearing a deep sound with your air. Compare inhalations with an open and closed throat and notice the dramatically different pitches created by the thin airflow as opposed to the thick airflow.

Now that your throat and back are in the proper position, you can work with your diaphragm, which is a strong muscle that causes the lungs to expand and contract. You must ensure that you use the diaphragm instead of the abdomen muscles when breathing. When you inhale, put your hand on your abdomen and feel it extend outward, as shown in fig. 23.1.

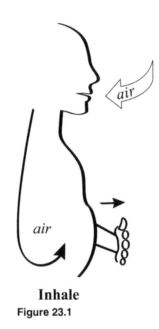

Inhale
Figure 23.1

Your rib cage should already be expanded to allow the air in without tension. Fill your lungs completely from the bottom up.

Exhaling

Exhaling is naturally the most important aspect of breathing for the wind player, since it activates the sound.

After inhaling, remain in the "inhale" position for a moment and establish the air pressure by briefly simulating the consonants "pff" and start blowing the air outward. While exhaling, make sure that you do *not* push the abdomen inward, even though it might seem to be a natural movement at first.

Concentrate on exhaling with the diaphragm instead of the abdominal muscles (see fig. 23.2). The abdomen muscles should remain fully expanded while the diaphragm pushes the air out of the lungs. Place your hand on your abdomen and make sure it stays in position rather than moving inward. Only at the end of the exhalation is it necessary to push the abdomen muscles in to let the remaining air out. The important aspect of this exercise is to gain control of the diaphragm.

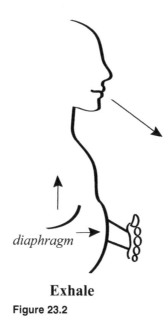

Exhale

Figure 23.2

While exhaling, it is practical to simulate the clarinet embouchure and thus expel the air fast and forward, as if actually playing. Good control of the diaphragm permits greater command of extreme dynamics, especially in the very soft dynamics.

SECRET 24: AIR MANAGEMENT

Proper management of airflow can enhance mental concentration. While teaching and practicing, I've noticed that the amount of note errors invariably increases when my students or I start running out of air at the ends of phrases.

Enhancing Mental Concentration with Air

An effective visualization technique is to regard each breath as oxygen nourishment for the blood. Rejuvenated blood enables the mind to better concentrate, whereas a shallow breath will hinder mental concentration. Make sure to breathe adequately before playing a difficult technical passage.

Experiment with this theory by breathing in halfway before playing an elaborate technical passage. Concentrate intensely to miss as few notes as possible. No matter how much you concentrate, you will likely notice more mistakes compared to when you played the same passage with your lungs filled with air.

Proper use of air while inhaling and exhaling greatly enhances performance on many levels. Positioning your body to allow the lungs to expand freely will maximize effectiveness.

Phrasing

Music is arranged in phrases much in the same way that a story is formed in sentences. When we read a book aloud, we take the appropriate pauses and breathe where necessary. The same should be done with a musical phrase.

Oxygenation

Breathing is also crucial for maintaining proper blood oxygenation. Avoid sustaining a musical line for too long simply to test if you "can make it to the end." Instead, keep your blood oxygenated by breathing where the music allows it. This will not only help your mental concentration, but it will also keep your airflow constant throughout the music. If you play until your lungs are empty, there will be a shortage of oxygen in the blood. When you breathe again, you will feel out of breath even though your lungs will be full of new air. It will take a few seconds for blood oxygenation to recover adequately to allow the next note to be played comfortably. Furthermore, if you inhale while old air is still in your lungs, you will breathe in oxygen on top of carbon dioxide and, again, you will feel out of breath even if your lungs are full of air.

Planning Breath Marks

Breathing is part of the musical phrase, and you need a plan that enhances the artistic result while keeping your body nourished with oxygen. Plan your breaths, write them in your music once you are certain of your musical decisions, and stick to your plan during the performance. In classical music, most phrases are formed in four-bar multiples (e.g., 4, 8, 12, 16). Some phrases are nearly impossible to complete without taking a breath, so it should be taken at a logical place, such as at the end of measure 8 in a 16-bar phrase. This allows the phrases to be symmetrical rather than sounding uneven. Proper air management will improve your mental concentration and allow you to achieve a fuller tone with less air.

Keep the Air Moving

Oftentimes, we are so intent on getting all the notes down when practicing fast technique that we forget to keep the air moving. The result may seem impressive technically, but the musical outcome is a robot-like performance. When you play notes, make sure you play *between* the notes as well. The more you keep your air moving and constantly vary its speed, the more musical your phrasing will be. Visualize the air movement between notes:

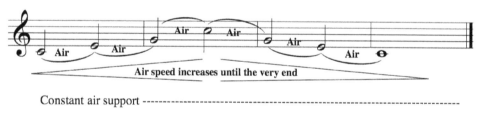

Figure 24.1

SECRET 25: THE STEREO EFFECT

There are several ways to tell if a clarinet tone is centered and contains all the desired characteristics of beauty, depth, and complexity. A critical performer is capable of judging these tonal aspects based on personal experience, training, taste, and musical context. Another way to determine if a tone is as centered and resonant as possible is to focus on how our ears actually *hear* the tone.

The Stereo Effect Exercise

The idea is to center the tone by making sure both ears perceive the sound equally well. (It is assumed here that the player's hearing is normal.) Play a note at a full dynamic. Upon careful listening, you might notice how one ear favors the tone more than the other. For example, the sound might seem louder in the left ear, and the theoretical result is a tone that is not centered, at least in our minds. By attempting to shift the tone toward the center so that both ears hear the sound equally well, we clarify our concept of a centered tone and make it more tangible.

While playing, balance the tone until the sound stimulates both eardrums equally, and, as a result, visualize and hear your tone becoming more and more centered. You will notice the sound becoming richer and fuller, and harmonics will become more obvious to the ear (see fig. 25.1). To enhance this experience, play this exercise in a dark room or with your eyes closed.

Play in all registers, taking the time to focus on how each eardrum picks up the sound waves. When both ears hear the sound at an equal intensity (when the stereo effect is achieved), the mind will become more aware of sound waves, and the musician will come to expect and create a richer tone.

Another way to be aware of the various harmonics within our tone is to notice how the eardrum physically reacts to it. For example, a pinched c^2 (two lines above the staff) will not stimulate the eardrum as intensely because many of the upper harmonics are absent. The tone will be thin and the eardrum will be comfortable hearing the simple, almost bare tone. When you release the bite, lower the pitch, and increase airflow, however, notice how the c^2 starts to have a piercing, almost uncomfortable effect on the eardrum.

After comparing both sounds, it is evident that the complexity and richness improves when harmonics are allowed to speak. The result is a rich and projecting tone.

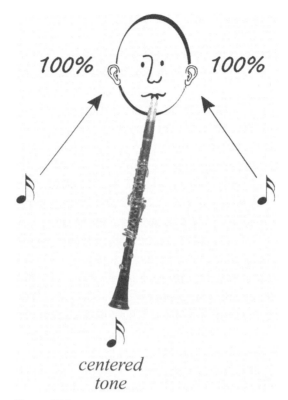

centered
tone

Figure 25.1

SECRET 26: DISSECTING TONE

Even the shortest note can be dissected and analyzed in detail. The shape of one note can vary a great deal, so it is important to recognize all its components. Whether a tone is long or short, loud or soft, accented or slurred, it can always be divided into three parts: attack (or beginning), duration (or sustain), and release (or ending, or decay). Electronic music specialists need to know these parameters to program and create various sounds with synthesizers. A multitude of combinations are possible, and being able to control each note's three components is imperative for a greater and more expressive sound palette.

There are many different ways of starting and ending a note. An attack or a release may be executed with the tongue or the air column, with more or less intensity, depending on the desired character. When playing a phrase, try to dissect each note until you can control each attack, duration, and release. Visualize the notes as shapes, and experiment with each tone's three variable parts.

Figure 26.1 illustrates different combination possibilities. For instance, the first note is a short eighth note starting and ending with the tongue, as indicated by the word "tongue" in the left and right margins. The middle (duration) section is actually very short, but it is there nevertheless. Example 2 (half note) starts and ends with the air column, although it very well could be played with a gentle tongue attack, if preferred. Example 3 can start and end with the tongue or air column, depending on the amount of intensity that is desired. Letters inside each shape suggest syllables to imagine while playing.

A note that starts or ends quickly is indicated as a square shape, and a longer attack or release is represented as either a round or arrowhead shape. The duration of the middle sections depends on the desired length of each note.

Examples 5 through 9 illustrate shape combinations with letters written as words at the end of each example. Additional combinations may be created, as well as other shapes. Diverse musical styles (folk music, jazz, and others) might use completely different sounds, so this technique is useful to assist the player in acquiring advanced listening skills to reproduce these varied sounds accurately.

Try playing one pitch in the different ways shown in the figure, and see if you can successfully make each distinct from another. Modify the three sections to create an array of contrasting note shapes. While playing an excerpt from a piece you know well, practice each note's three parts to see if the desired effect is indeed created.

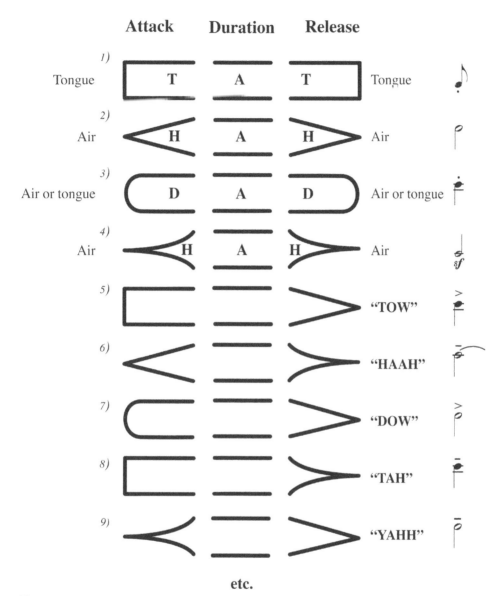

Figure 26.1

SECRET 27: PRACTICE TONE VS. CONCERT TONE

When we are practicing a challenging piece of music, it is tempting to concentrate mostly on the notes and neglect other important factors such as tone and phrasing. The result is often what I call a "practice" tone.

I would like to think that no matter what our stage of development is on a particular piece, we still want to play it as if we were performing onstage in a concert setting. I call this type of fully resonating tone a "concert tone."

A concert tone contains many harmonics, is devoid of any extra air noises, and is controlled with the diaphragm muscles. A good exercise to test the diaphragm-controlled airflow is to play a long note decrescendo in the clarion register without the lower fundamental note sounding. Contrary to popular belief, the softer you play, the *stronger* (or faster) the air pressure should be. If the air pressure dissipates too soon, the reed will vibrate more slowly and produce a lower note, resulting in the infamous "grunting" sound caused by a slower reed vibration. The reed needs sufficient air pressure to vibrate at a fast enough speed to produce clean clarion and high notes.

When playing the decrescendo, think in terms of numbers: descending numbers for the dynamic itself, and ascending numbers for the air pressure or speed. The dynamic numbers also help in playing softer in a smooth, gradual manner (fig. 27.1).

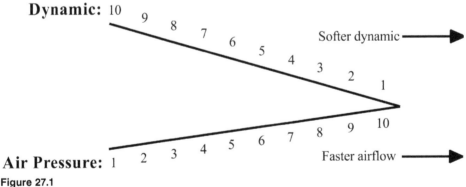

Figure 27.1

Another helpful tone exercise is to practice different dynamic combinations while making sure that the *pianissimo* notes are as soft as possible without any airy sound whatsoever. Again, use the diaphragm to maintain strong air pressure. Begin soft notes with very fast airflow in order for the reed to vibrate fast enough to allow high notes to sound clearly, as shown in fig. 27.2.

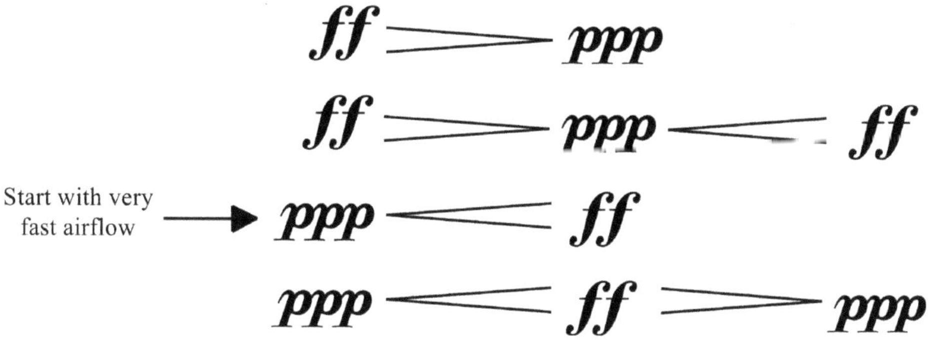

$$ff \mathrel{\Large>\!\!\!=} ppp$$

$$ff \mathrel{\Large>\!\!\!=} ppp \mathrel{\Large=\!\!\!<} ff$$

Start with very
fast airflow $\longrightarrow$ $ppp \mathrel{\Large=\!\!\!<} ff$

$$ppp \mathrel{\Large=\!\!\!<} ff \mathrel{\Large>\!\!\!=} ppp$$

Figure 27.2

Creating Your Own Concert Hall Resonance in the Practice Room

Acoustics in a good concert hall may significantly enhance one's tone. To simulate sound decay naturally occurring in a large concert hall, develop a habit of not ending your notes abruptly. Instead, add a virtually unnoticeable decay to the end of notes, except for extremely short accents. See fig. 27.3.

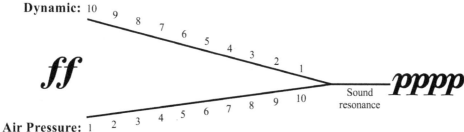

Dynamic: 10 9 8 7 6 5 4 3 2 1

ff

Sound resonance *pppp*

Air Pressure: 1 2 3 4 5 6 7 8 9 10

Figure 27.3

SECRET 28: TONE SHOPPING

No matter how much one might wish to imitate the tone of a favorite clarinetist, all musicians have their own unique sound. How wonderful it is that someone's "voice" cannot be exactly reproduced by another human being!

The idea of tone shopping implies that a good tone can be turned into a great tone if each note's timbre is carefully thought out beforehand. With tone shopping, players personalize their tone by choosing the nuances that turn it into the most rich and beautiful sound possible.

To find our "best voice," we must first search for it and experiment with various tone colors before making a final choice. The tone shopping exercise allows you to maximize the beauty of a sound and to develop tone awareness in order for all notes to match one another across all registers.

Play a long tone on low E. Using the stereo-effect concept described in Secret 25: The Stereo Effect, center the sound and make sure the tone rings with enough partials. Vary characteristics such as air speed, embouchure, and tongue position until you achieve the desired tone quality. Similarly, follow with a long tone on low F. Search for the best possible tone on both notes. Then play both notes back and forth until they match perfectly. Continue with a long tone on low F♯ and proceed as before, until E, F, and F♯ are perfectly matched. Continue the exercise using all notes of the chromatic scale in ascending order until all notes match one another with the best tone possible throughout all registers.

Naturally, this exercise should be executed with patience in order to be able to hear tonal subtleties. This should be practiced diligently about twenty or thirty minutes a day without hurrying the outcome by attempting to fix each note in a single practice session. The first day could be dedicated to only one octave, or even half that amount, if necessary.

The advantage of taking enough time to do quality work with tone shopping is that after a few weeks of daily practice, the exercise need not be repeated in the future as you will automatically resort to your memory to produce each tone as flawlessly as possible.

After this technique is mastered, your primary tone will become consistent, and you can then build upon it to develop greater tonal variety. It is a good idea to develop a solid, reliable tone so that you are able to modify it at will when necessary. Contrasting musical styles require different tonal characteristics, and if your sound palette is even, you will be able to achieve control of changeable details such as vibrato, tone color, harmonic shading, tonal presence, and personality.

An important variation of this exercise is to play small and large intervals rather than consecutive notes. Work on evenness of tone with a focus on tone color, depth, and pitch accuracy. Notice how some registers will require more or less air speed to match one another. For example, to match low E with c³, the low E must be played with substantial airflow to sound as present and full as the c³. Low notes naturally project less, whereas high notes resonate loudly easily.

It is up to the performer to gain a complete understanding of the unique properties of a clarinet tone in order to balance and match each register, depending on the given dynamic, musical style, and phrasing. Tone shopping is just the tool to achieve this goal.

SECRET 29: PRINTING SOUND INTO MEMORY

Do you listen to recordings of your favorite clarinetists on a regular basis? Not only does this practice allow you to be inspired by their diverse performance styles, but it also is a very efficient way to learn about tone.

In order to develop a beautiful clarinet tone, one's ears must first hear and internalize the desired tone before it can be reproduced on the instrument. If a clarinetist only has a vague idea of what a satisfactory tone may be, chances are that it will be challenging to create a good tone.

All clarinetists aim for beauty of tone, and each player will eventually find his or her own unique "voice" on the instrument. Before reaching that goal, however, I believe it is necessary to develop an internal palette of sonorities to successfully emulate a chosen tone color.

I suggest listening to a wide variety of recorded clarinet performances. In addition to expanding repertoire knowledge, this allows you to formulate more clearly the kind of tone that suits your personal preference.

Once you find the performers who possess the kind of sonority you favor, I suggest listening to each recording numerous times so the various tones are "recorded" in the brain for future reference. By "many times," I mean several dozen times each week for several weeks, until the tones reach the subconscious mind and are permanently memorized.

When this is achieved, select a tone that will best fit the musical style of the piece you are practicing (I always appreciate a soloist who has the ability to intrigue an audience by expressing a multitude of clarinet sounds within one recital).

While you are playing, your ear will tell your body what to do to create the sound you internalized. This will prove more powerful than a teacher trying to explain in detail how to manipulate the embouchure or airflow. If you have a particular sound in your internal memory bank, your embouchure and airflow will eventually execute the movements instinctively, and you will achieve the desired tone more effectively.

For example, when performing Brahms, one might prefer using a dark sound resembling that of a German clarinetist. Naturally, no performer can ever (nor would want to) sound like someone else, but the sound concept is etched in the memory, and therefore helps the process of formulating a desired tone. Every player sounds unique, which is one of the most exciting aspects of performance. However, listening to different clarinet masters is inspiring.

When your memory contains a rich collection of sound colors and ideas, you will eventually be able to better reproduce these sounds. Therefore, it is a good practice to be particularly alert when listening to great clarinet performances so that your plan of reproducing these sounds can go forward. Use different tone colors for different time periods or styles, and allow yourself to experiment with techniques such as vibrato to vary the sound (see Secret 95: Vibrato).

Finally, it is imperative to be comfortable with your equipment when working on tone. Be sure that your mouthpiece and reed combination (and instrument) allow free airflow, clean articulation, accurate intonation, and good projection.

SECRET 30: IMPROVING EMBOUCHURE ENDURANCE

It is entirely possible to have a big and dark tone with a soft reed. Reeds that are too hard can result in a wonderfully full tone; however, soft dynamics may become airy and difficult to produce.

Equipment

A strong embouchure is required to provide the stamina needed to perform major pieces without fatigue. Choosing the right equipment can help improve embouchure endurance in several ways:

Practice with Softer Reeds

Softer reeds might initially seem too easy to play and result in a thin and brittle sound. However, with practice you will notice that your air management becomes more efficient, resulting in a full and pure tone. No air will escape through the bore without first being processed by the reed, and there will no longer be extra "air noise" in your tone. An analogy would be to compare a basic compact car with a high-performance car. A car built to reach a maximum speed of 100 mph will probably be overworked at 80 mph. However, if you drive a sports car designed to reach 150 mph, the ride at 80 mph will feel smooth and effortless.

Playing a softer reed will require adjustments on your part in terms of air pressure, air management, and embouchure control. At first, you may not like your tone. Avoid biting the reed and play with a tuner to ensure you are not getting sharp. Practice long tones, scales, pieces, orchestral or band excerpts, and your usual repertoire. Later, try gradually increasing reed strength, if needed. With patience, your embouchure and airflow will adjust, and eventually you might wonder why you ever played harder reeds.

Experiment with Various Mouthpiece and Reed Combinations

Your setup might be more resistant than necessary. Depending on personal physiology, a mouthpiece with a medium facing and a medium or medium-soft reed may work better than a long facing with a hard reed, or vice versa. The idea is to have a good, solid, full tone without having to strain to overcome excessive resistance.

Teeth Cushion

Cover your lower teeth with a small, soft, and flexible protective pad, such as EZO® denture cushions. This can help improve embouchure endurance by providing protection for the lower lip (see Secret 82: EZO Teeth Cushion).

Practice in Increments

Instead of playing until your embouchure gets too tired, try practicing for twenty minutes, then resting for twenty minutes, and repeat the sequence. The down time can be used productively with music theory, memorization, or sight-singing exercises. After a few days, decrease your rest time by practicing twenty-five minutes and stopping for only ten minutes. Eventually, extend your practice to twenty-eight minutes, followed by two minutes of rest.

This process takes patience, but by extending your playing time in small increments, you will be able to monitor your progress and eventually your body will teach you what you need to do to improve endurance. To help keep track of your time increments, you can find an online countdown stopwatch at Online-Stopwatch.com, or you can use a stopwatch feature or app on your device.

Oxygenating Embouchure Muscles

Musicians should follow the example set by top athletes by keeping their muscles supplied with plenty of oxygen. After playing for a long period of time, the lip and chin muscles build up tension and toxins, restricting local blood circulation and causing embouchure fatigue. Allowing blood circulation to return to normal will oxygenate the muscles and increase their performance and your endurance. Air leaking from the sides of your mouth can be an indication that you need a short break. It is important to take the reed away from the embouchure for a few seconds during rests to allow the constricted blood vessels to return to normal. Make a conscious effort to recuperate during rests in the music. Rather than simply counting empty bars, gently move the lip muscles to increase the blood flow.

Rest

Rest and avoid stress before concerts, rehearsals, and private lessons. Plan your day so you will arrive refreshed and ready for the task. Patience is key, so allow at least one month before deciding if these strategies help.

SECRET 31: KNOT IN TONE

In order to play with a full and rich tone with relative ease, it is necessary to be able to produce the entire spectrum of tone dynamics beforehand. By practicing extreme dynamics, one can ultimately play regular dynamics with a full tone and without excessive effort.

Figure 31.1 represents a long tone played in a crescendo, reaching the ideal "core" (knot in tone) and extending beyond that to an extreme dynamic level at which the tone would actually distort.

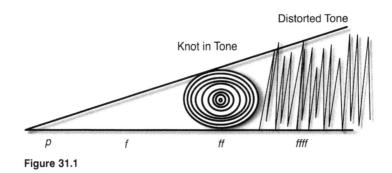

Figure 31.1

To practice this exercise, increase the volume of a long tone until distortion occurs (this takes a considerable amount of effort in terms of air support). Repeat this exercise and, this time, stop the tone just before distortion occurs. Listen to the fullness of tone and try to achieve a full tone ("knot") with less effort than when you played the distorted tone. As you practice, your efficiency will improve and you will notice that it will take less and less effort to reach a full tone.

SECRET 32: PLAYING WITH FIRE

Of all instruments, the clarinet can best voice a note quietly, make it swell, decrease, and fade away. Hence its amazing ability to produce a distant sound, the echo of an echo, a sound like twilight.

—Hector Berlioz, French composer; from his *Treatise on Instrumentation and Orchestration*, 1843

A common challenge when playing a note decrescendo is to decay completely without any air noise. As you decrease the dynamic and amount of air, you must *increase* the speed of the air. When you end a soft note, end it with the diaphragm instead of biting the reed with the jaw. If you slow down your air while decaying, the reed will stop vibrating, resulting in extra air noise. A good way to practice increasing air speed in a soft dynamic is to play with fire. I am always pleased when I find out my students do not know how to operate a lighter (this means they do not smoke). Here is a productive way to use a lighter:

1. Hold the lighter in your hand and extend your arm as straight as possible.
2. Flick the lighter to light the flame.
3. With your arm extended, quickly blow out the flame.
4. With your arm still extended, blow at the flame but this time, focus your air in a thin line like a laser beam and push the flame lightly without blowing it out (see fig. 32.1).
5. Increase the speed of your air until you blow out the flame. You will notice it took more air speed to blow it out when your air was concentrated like a laser beam.
6. Emulate this feeling on the clarinet when you play decrescendo.

Figure 32.1

Practicing blowing out the flame with a concentrated airstream will improve your tone as you decrease the dynamic. Never let your sound become airy. Keep it full and resonant, especially in soft dynamics.

SECRET 33: THE TONE IS RINGING!

For the first few years of training, clarinetists can bite on the reed without noticing the effects it has on tone and intonation. This is because even with biting, a clarinet tone can sound clean, clear, and pleasant to less experienced players. However, once the ear matures and craves greater complexity of tone, perceptions can change drastically.

Playing with a silent tuner on "needle" mode that displays pitch placement is useful; however, I believe that intonation is best corrected by the *ear* rather than by the *eye*. For this reason, I advocate practicing with a tuner drone sounding in the background. An effective approach is to play a scale against a continuous drone. While you change notes, correct and adjust each *interval* rather than simply correcting each individual note. Notice the distance between notes, much as string players do.

You may become aware that many notes in the clarion are quite sharp, such as d^1 and $d\sharp^1$ (fourth line on staff) and g^1 (top of the staff). Significant adjustments will have to be made with the jaw to correct these notes consistently. Lowering the jaw will help flatten the pitch and create more room for airflow. This embouchure shift may take a while to internalize, but with practice, when the ear anticipates a flatter pitch, the body will follow with the correct jaw position.

Harmonics and the Eardrum

Biting on the reed results in the upper harmonics being squeezed away, leaving the tone with a simple quality and sharp intonation. When playing a note with the jaw in a lower position and with more airflow, notice the pitch flattening and hear the added resonance and complexity in your tone. For example, play a c^2 (two lines above the staff) with a squeezed embouchure followed by playing the c^2 with an open jaw. Notice how the ear almost "rattles" or "rings" when the pitch is lower. The new harmonics created by an unrestricted embouchure and airflow add interesting complexity to the tone, resulting in a ringing of the eardrum. In short, if your ear is not ringing when you are playing in the clarion and high registers, harmonics are missing and chances are your intonation is sharp.

A visual exercise with color can be used to illustrate complexity of tone. Look at a white object and make yourself aware of how your eyes react to the simple and basic color. Then look at a bright, neon pink or lime green object. Notice how your eye is stimulated by the color complexity and how more noticeable the object is to the eye. The many colors contained in the neon make the eyes "work" harder, just as the ear processes more sound elements with a tone that contains harmonics. Pay attention to your eardrums and how they react to tone. When the tone is ringing, the fun begins.

SECRET 34: STOPWATCH LONG TONES

Practicing long tones correctly and efficiently allows you to play longer musical phrases with fewer breaths. One way to maximize air management, airflow efficiency, and embouchure endurance is to practice long tones with a stopwatch. Choosing a digital stopwatch (as opposed to an analog or mechanical stopwatch) will simplify your timekeeping.

You can find an easy-to-use online stopwatch at Online-Stopwatch.com or by searching various stopwatch sites online. You can also use the stopwatch feature on your device. The following exercise is not only helpful in improving your air management, it's also very fun. First, test how long you can hold a medium-soft note and write down the timing.

Once you have measured your longest timing, perform the following exercise: Do a long tone for ten seconds. Follow with another long tone, but this time, add one second, for a total of eleven seconds. Take a few slow, deep breaths between each long tone and start again, continuing with twelve seconds, thirteen seconds, and so on. Make sure not to skip increments (even though you might feel ready to do so right away), and breathe from the bottom up for maximum air intake. Each time you succeed in adding a one-second increment, write down the new timing to record your progress. A good goal is to reach about thirty-five seconds. Ambitious players may try for about forty-five seconds after a few days of practice.

You can use the boxes shown in fig. 34.1 to monitor your progress or create your own numbering system in a practice journal.

Figure 34.1

If you do the exercise with one-second increments, the gradual increase in tone length will be so minimal that your body will have a chance to adjust and inadvertently improve air management in the process. Additionally, your embouchure strength will gradually improve.

Play long tones on all notes in each register and try to reach the longest time possible (without overdoing it or feeling uncomfortable), keeping in mind to use the proper breathing techniques described in Secret 23: Breathing. The tone should be clean and even, without extra air noise. Use reeds that respond well in soft dynamics and that are not too hard.

Try to add at least fifteen to twenty seconds to the tone length you noted on your first day. Long tones' maximum duration can vary depending on individual abilities; however, a total of about thirty-five to forty seconds is a typical limit. To increase lung capacity, sit with a straight back with one leg slightly lower than the other. Standing up is another option.

After two or three weeks, test your improvement by practicing long solos such as the slow movements from Rachmaninov's Second Symphony and Beethoven's Seventh Symphony or any slow movements from your solo, chamber, or ensemble repertoire. Practice slow excerpts or pieces over and over, and you will notice how the effort level will decrease over time, much like an athlete training for a marathon. A good way to document your progress is to create a small journal dedicated to long tones. Write the date of each practice and the longest timing of each note you achieved that day.

SECRET 35: ELIMINATING CRACKING IN HIGH REGISTERS

One of the most annoying things clarinetists face is the *grunt* (or subtone) that occasionally appears in the clarion and high registers, especially when articulating or when playing very softly.

Dr. Phillip O. Paglialonga, clarinet professor at Virginia Tech University and author of *Squeak Big: Practical Fundamentals for the Successful Clarinetist*, offers advice on how to eliminate cracking in high registers.

> Cracking in the clarion and high registers is the symptom of a very simple problem: the reed is not vibrating fast enough to produce a high pitch. As a result, the performer is often left to compensate in some other way for the note to speak at all. Frequently, this involves severely biting upward into the reed or changing the basic tongue position. Unfortunately, these compensations have serious downsides, which ultimately become problematic."

> Few orchestral passages terrify clarinetists as much as the solo in Respighi's *Pines of Rome*, shown in fig. 35.1. Too often, players experience a grunt or subtone as they diminuendo to nothing and the effect of the phrase is lost.

Respighi's *Pines of Rome Clarinet Solo*

Figure 35.1

> A solution is to make sure the right thumb always pushes the mouthpiece slightly into the upper teeth in an upward direction, resulting in slightly more reed in the mouth. This also helps ensure that the clarinet is securely placed in the mouth and adds more structure to the basic sound by stabilizing the mouthpiece.

> When making a delicate diminuendo, gently push the mouthpiece up into the teeth and keep the air relaxed. Be mindful that nothing changes except the faster speed of the air as you make the diminuendo. No other embouchure manipulations should be necessary.

> With a little practice you will find that this technique helps to control the high registers and allows the execution of the perfect decrescendo without cracking notes.

QUICK-TIPS BULLETIN BOARD—TONE

- Avoid puffing the cheeks when playing, as it reduces embouchure control.
- In order to play with the best tone possible, imagine you are dressing it up in a concert outfit and avoid playing with a "practice tone."
- Avoid air leaks at the sides of the mouth. Think of gluing the "wet" part of the inside of your lip corners together.
- If you have a problem with a note (squeaking, cracking, intonation, or response), concentrate on perfecting the previous note, as the end of this note is the beginning of the next note.
- Avoid ending your notes with extra air noise. Keep the airflow moving to allow the reed to vibrate and the sound to remain resonant until the very end.
- When playing soft dynamics, be sure to project your tone. Compare this to an actor whispering a secret on stage during a play, which is very different from whispering a secret on film where microphones amplify the sound or in real life when a secret is told softly and directly into a person's ear. The actor facing a live audience needs to speak louder in order to be heard at the back of the hall. The same is true for a wind instrument. When playing softly, keep projecting the airflow speed, especially in decrescendos.
- A full and resonant clarinet tone has a core (or center), surrounded by an outer envelope of overtones. I like to compare a beautiful clarinet tone to the parts of a tree. The tree's cylindrical trunk, with water and nutrients flowing through it, represents the center of the clarinet tone. The protective bark represents the harmonics surrounding the tone's center and figuratively holds the tone together. This illustrates how important it is to keep the tone centered with no excessive edge escaping through the "bark." This analogy helps one to recognize the adjustments necessary to create a warmer and more vibrant tone.

CHAPTER 4

Technical Strategies

SECRET 36: NATURAL FINGER MOTION

Although clarinet playing may not necessarily always involve natural body movements, it is important to study and analyze natural hand motions to adapt them to the instrument. A relaxed and natural approach will reduce the tendency to tighten the hand and arm muscles during rapid technical passages.

If one holds out a relaxed hand and bends the wrist as illustrated in fig. 36.1, it is easy to see how the fingers naturally curve and become rounded. After practicing the three hand motions on both hands several times, hold the clarinet while maintaining the final, curved hand position. Similarly, each individual finger naturally curves and should move accordingly on the clarinet keys (see fig. 36.2).

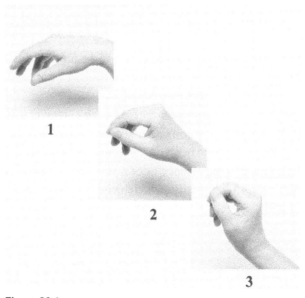

Figure 36.1

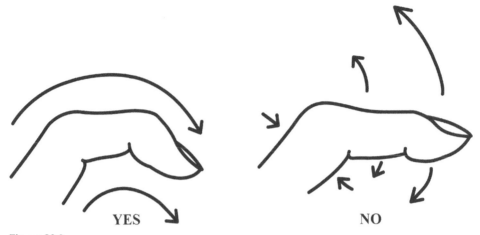

Figure 36.2

Practice slow scales in front of the mirror, making sure the fingers do not become stiff, extended, or straightened. At times, this may feel as though the hands and fingers are going through complete retraining. The initial discomfort might cause you to take a "shortcut" and return to your previous hand and finger positions; however, slow and patient work will yield a much more fluid technique and perhaps prevent future injury.

While practicing slow scales in front of the mirror, move each finger from the first joint (at the base of the hand) and imagine that the rest of the finger is somewhat "asleep" or extremely relaxed. In this way, the first finger joint will guide the rest of the finger and the natural weight of each finger will be used to cover holes or close keys. This technique will help avoid excess pressure on tone holes and keys.

Continue the exercise by playing increasingly faster scales (still in front of the mirror), and vary technical patterns (such as thirds or octaves) by lifting two, three, or more fingers simultaneously.

Try playing various trills to test how relaxed each finger is while moving rapidly. Remember to relax the arms and shoulders as well as the fingers, and refrain from caving in the finger joints when covering holes or closing keys.

The light feeling you will experience after a few days of practice will give you the impression that each finger gently gets detached from the hand while playing, especially during trills.

SECRET 37: THE HAT TRICK FOR SCALES

The study of scales will solve a greater number of technical problems in a shorter amount of time than the study of any other technical exercise.

—Andrés Segovia, Spanish classical guitarist

Scales are the building blocks of technique and they are present in virtually every musical phrase we play, whether they are ascending, descending, or in various patterns such as thirds or arpeggios. The most important scales to learn are all major scales: C, D, E, F, G, A, B, C♯ (or D♭), D♯ (or E♭), F♯ (or G♭), G♯ (or A♭), B♭, and all harmonic, melodic, and natural minor scales. It is one thing to learn scales and read them out of a scale book, and it is another to actually memorize all the patterns. Clarinet scales can be quite challenging, especially because the range is so wide with almost four octaves to conquer, and because the register key produces an interval of a twelfth instead of an octave. A fun way to facilitate learning and memorizing scales is to learn them in random order by following these six steps:

1. Cut small pieces of paper and write one scale name on each piece. Depending on which scales you are working on, include major scales and harmonic, melodic, and natural minor scales. For example, write "C major," "a minor harmonic," "f minor melodic," and so on.
2. Put all pieces of paper in a hat.
3. Pick a piece of paper at random and read the scale name. Before playing it, think it through, formulate the pattern in your mind, then play it.
4. If you play the scale with some errors, put the piece of paper back in the hat.
5. If you play the scale perfectly, remove the piece of paper from the hat.
6. Do this exercise until the hat is empty.☺

SECRET 38: THE HALF-HOLE EXERCISE FOR WIDE INTERVALS

Wide intervals often sound uneven or bumpy, especially from low notes to high notes. To play such leaps more smoothly, gradually uncover the top of the left index finger tone hole, ultimately leaving most of the hole surface uncovered. Keep the finger curved and rotate the wrist downward.

Although the term "half-hole" is used here, the reality is that in order to prevent flatness of pitch, the index finger should eventually uncover most of the tone hole rather than leaving half of it covered. The index finger should not "slide" down the hole. Instead, it should pivot so the air can escape more progressively, creating a pure and gentle interval leap. If the index finger inadvertently slides down instead of pivoting, the air will be allowed to escape too quickly and result in a sudden, louder high note. The left index finger should pivot rather than sliding down, as shown in fig. 38.1.

Figure 38.1

Notice how the bottom of the index fingertip acts as a door hinge by resting on the bottom of the metal ring, never dislodging itself or sliding down. This enables the fingertip to reposition itself comfortably and smoothly on the tone hole when needed.

Play the following exercise very slowly. Start with the bottom note, slur to the clarion note with the register key, and simply pivot the left index fingertip (at ◡ sign). Decrease the dynamic at the end of each bar.

Figure 38.2

In order to simplify this exercise in the beginning stage of practice, it is not necessary to add the G♯/d♯[1] key on the third note of each bar (the key is usually added to correct intonation on high notes starting on d[2]). The G♯/d♯[1] key should be added as soon as the half-hole movement becomes comfortable (of course, the key may be omitted depending on the intonation characteristics of a specific instrument). Eventually, the exercise can be played much faster.

A similar technique may be done with the left thumb *instead* of the left index finger, especially for high e[2]. The difference is that the thumb hole should be opened from the bottom, and only a small fraction of the hole should be uncovered.

Interestingly, the index finger can also act as an acoustic "shock absorber" when a gentle and soft attack is required in the high register. For example, before playing a high d[2], coordinate the index half-hole movement with the beginning of the air attack. Breathe, and as you start blowing to begin the note, simultaneously place (or gently "pop") the index fingertip on the bottom of the left index finger ring. Why this works is still a matter of opinion, but one theory is that the placement of the finger reminds the player to establish the air pressure properly in order for the high note to come out gently and effortlessly.

SECRET 39: HALF-HOLE THUMB

I have found two interesting ways to use the half-hole thumb technique. First, it can help execute a perfect half-step trill between throat b♭ and B or a whole-step trill between throat a and B. Second, it can help improve the response of the high register beginning with d² (third space above the staff).

A–B Trill

Play a b¹ (third line on the staff), with the right little finger on the right b¹ key. While keeping this fingering, slightly uncover the left thumb hole, and press on the throat a key. Remain in this position and simply lift both index fingers simultaneously up and down to create a flawless trill.

B♭–A Trill

Play a b¹ and while keeping this fingering, uncover the left thumb hole slightly, and press on the throat a and b♭ key. As with the a–b¹ trill, remain in this position and lift both index fingers simultaneously up and down. The hidden advantage of practicing this exercise is that it will inevitably improve your left index finger technique by keeping the tip of the finger near the hole without reaching high on the throat a key. Your intervals will sound smoother and easier to play.

High Register Response

As seen in Secret 38: The Half-Hole Exercise for Wide Intervals, the half-hole exercise with the left index finger is an efficient way to execute smooth wide intervals up to the high register. Instead of using the left index finger, try doing the half-hole with the thumb and see if it accomplishes a similar or better result (see fig. 39.1).

Figure 39.1

SECRET 40: LEFT INDEX FINGER

A major challenge on the clarinet is achieving a smooth "break" or clean transition between throat a, and clarion b¹. The left index finger plays an important role in accomplishing this smoothly. The most common mistake is to stretch and straighten this finger when going through the break, thus creating "travel distance" between the throat a key and the left index finger tone hole (f♯). Since the clarinet is unique in its design and requires much attention from the left index finger, it is important to position that digit correctly. As opposed to a recorder, where the fingers only need to cover individual tone holes, the clarinetist plays several keys with each finger. The left index finger plays the a♭ side key, the front a key, and the first upper tone hole, f♯. The fingers must be prepared to play all these positions at any moment so they must *mold* to these keys. Curl the left index finger so it touches all three areas (throat a, a♭, and f♯), and do not straighten it when playing other notes. Instead, move the wrist in a circular fashion without any tension, as shown in fig. 40.1.

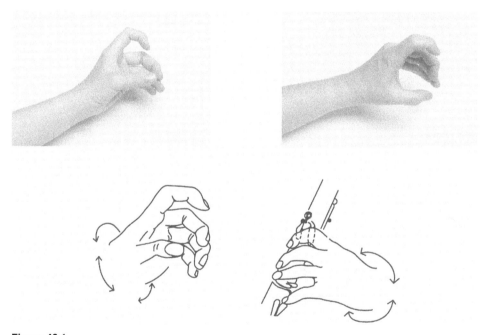

Figure 40.1

The index finger is curved and stays near the f♯ tone hole while the wrist rotates when playing throat a♭, a, and f♯ as shown in figure 40.2.

In fig. 40.3, the left index finger remains curved and moves from the first joint only (as shown on the left side). Relax the first joint, and press gently on the keys

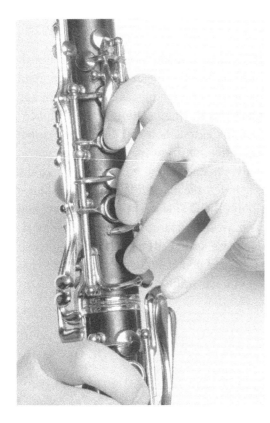

Figure 40.2

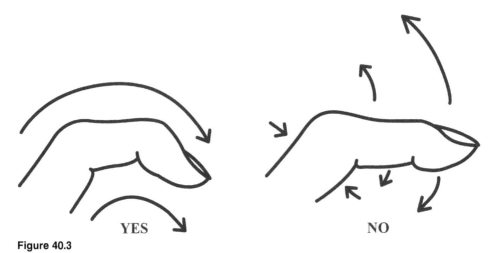

YES   NO

Figure 40.3

or f♯ tone hole. Do not straighten the second or third joints; doing so will create tension (as shown on the right).

The exercise in fig. 40.4 is designed to help keep the left index finger curved. Play f♯–a♭–f♯–a♭ *without* removing the index finger from the f♯ tone hole. In the same manner, play f-a-f-a, while keeping the "f" fingering down. The intonation will be affected, but here we want to focus on finger action. Play e-a-e-a, and so on. Always keep the f♯, f, e, and e♭ fingerings down while alternately playing a, a, and b♭.

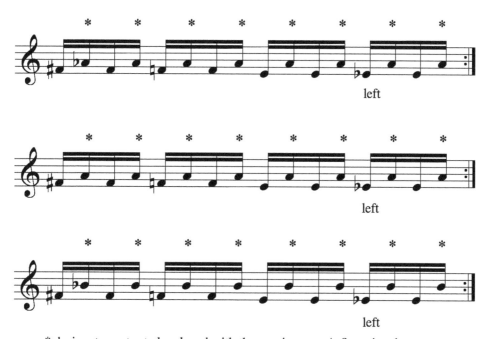

* designates notes to be played with the previous note's fingering down

Figure 40.4

SECRET 41: LITTLE FINGER

An unusual technical problem for clarinetists is that the least strong and smallest fingers are the ones doing most of the work. On the soprano Boehm clarinet, the little fingers can each activate four keys, whereas most other fingers operate only one or two keys. Tension in the little fingers can cause the ring fingers to inadvertently open holes, resulting in squeaking. The natural and curved position of each finger allows a relaxed and comfortable movement.

Figure 41.1

It is most effective to move the little fingers from the first joint nearest the hand and use the weight of each finger to close the keys instead of pushing them down forcefully. Some clarinetists may ultimately choose to use one side over the other (right or left little finger), depending on natural preference and ability. Play the exercise in fig. 41.2 a 12th down (written *up a 12th* to avoid ledger lines; the first note of the exercise is low A♭).

Notice that the pattern is to be played with the right little finger, and then repeated with the left little finger (except for the A♭/e♭¹ key, which can be played only on the right side on the traditional Boehm system).

Start slowly, and gradually increase the tempo. Eliminate "blips" or "in-between" notes by carefully analyzing where and why errors occur. Correct them by either closing down one key or tone hole earlier, or opening a key or tone hole earlier, depending on the problem. Repeat the first line several times until it is flawless, then move on to the next line. For best results, memorize the entire exercise.

Figure 41.2

SECRET 42: PERFECTING THE CHROMATIC SCALE

One of the most important foundations of a solid technique on any instrument is the chromatic scale. It is important to master the scale upward and downward with various fingerings. For example, the scale in fig. 42.1 may start either with the right or left little finger, and the f♯ (first space on the staff) may be played either with the left index finger or with the left thumb and two trill keys on the right.

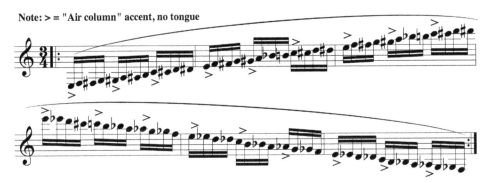

Figure 42.1

It is easy to fall into the habit of rushing this scale and inadvertently skipping notes or playing unevenly. For this reason, I suggest practicing this vital scale slowly with a metronome. One way to make sure that each note will be allotted equal time and importance is to play sixteenth notes with *very noticeable* breath or air accents at the beginning of each beat. The accents should be played with the air column instead of the tongue.

Initially, play each accent extremely loudly and play softly on the remaining notes. Admittedly, at this point the exercise will sound quite harsh and less than artistic, but the object is to carve a pattern in the mind that will act as a constant and reliable frame. Accents are played on E, G♯, and C in all octaves.

Focusing on the accented notes will enable you to play the remaining notes in a gentle and flowing manner while maintaining a solid technical and rhythmic foundation on each beat. Increase the speed gradually, and continue to play accents on each beat. When perfect evenness is achieved, play all notes without accents, but do keep the accents in mind to prevent technical inaccuracies.

After practicing this exercise for several days, you should notice a dramatic improvement in technical evenness in *all* scale patterns, including diatonic scales, arpeggios, and so forth.

After mastering the chromatic scale, it is helpful to break the scale down into different patterns such as chromatic minor thirds, chromatic perfect fourths, and other more complex chromatic patterns. To vary, play chromatic scales starting on different notes.

For detailed chromatic exercises, see Secret 51: Developing Technical Independence.

SECRET 43: PERFECTING THE HIGH REGISTER

There are a number of problems to conquer while playing a chromatic passage in the high register. The fingerings are often complex, and they can also result in intonation discrepancies and tone unevenness.

Naturally, the goal is to play a chromatic passage perfectly in tune with matching tone colors, and with the simplest fingerings possible. I find that the exercise in fig. 43.1 brings all these ideals to life. It also allows the high $g\sharp^3$ to be played with extreme ease, whereas many intermediate players stop at high g^3. Play the passage in the figure with the fingerings indicated.

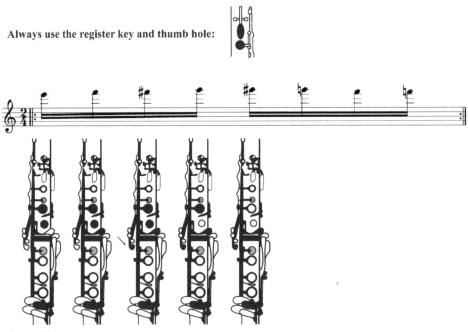

Figure 43.1

Notice that only *one* finger moves for each fingering change. For this exercise, moving more than one finger at a time is incorrect. One way to easily memorize the fingerings is to think (going upward from e^3) of adding one key (on the left), then another key (on the right), then opening a hole (left ring finger), then opening another hole (middle finger), that is, think to open: "key-key, hole-hole." The opposite is done with closing holes and keys going downward: think to close: "hole-hole, key-key."

Be sure to blow steadily, flatten the chin, and slightly move the jaw forward so the highest notes will sound resonant and not flat.

Another way to improve high register technique is to practice a diatonic pattern in C major, followed by the same pattern in various keys. Play the pattern in C major, then add one sharp, then one flat, then two sharps, and so on.

I suggest starting out by playing each note with an accent, and moving the fingers almost in a robot-like manner to "print" and separate each note mentally. The fingerings listed on the previous page are excellent for diatonic passages, as well as thirds and other intervals. I do not recommend them for most arpeggios and large leaps, however. The above fingerings match very well within scales, but they lack the extra brilliance needed in certain passages such as a *f* arpeggio at the end of a concerto. The exercise in fig. 43.2 allows you to master any combination of these suggested fingerings.

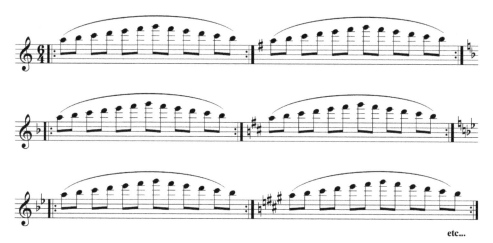

etc...

Figure 43.2

SECRET 44: PLAY AIR CLARINET

Do you remember your younger years when you would do carefree things like playing air guitar? Playing an imaginary instrument can be fun and while it has little to do with the reality of playing an instrument, the concept can be useful.

With this in mind, imagine playing air clarinet. Instead of pressing on the keys forcefully during technically challenging runs, envision your clarinet is as light as air and gently float your fingers over your instrument.

One exercise is to play challenging technical passages *without* blowing into your instrument and listen for any key noise. Put your instrument in your mouth, but do not let any notes sound so you can concentrate on finger technique exclusively. Challenging technical passages can sometimes result in tension, so it is helpful to practice technique without the added component of blowing.

The excerpts from Mozart's clarinet concerto shown in fig. 44.1 all contain tricky passages. Gently practice each line until you can play through them with absolutely no noise. This will result in less tension and lighter finger technique.

Bar 83

Bars 110-11

Bars 148-49
Figure 44.1

Another helpful exercise is to practice in front of a mirror and see if you can keep your instrument perfectly still while you play. This will allow you to develop more awareness and adopt the habit of playing with lighter fingers. Thereafter, play with normal movement.

Once these two concepts of eliminating key noise and immobilizing your instrument are mastered, your finger dexterity will improve, and you will be glad you went down memory lane.

SECRET 45: THE STICK ON A FENCE

Playing each and every note clearly and accurately in fast, technically difficult passages can be a real challenge for clarinetists and instrumentalists in general. A good analogy might be to compare this performance issue to that of reading a textbook more quickly than your brain can comprehend the words. The result can be that one misses important points. Playing technical passages at tempos beyond our capabilities results in loss of some of the meaning and effect of the music. A similar comparison can be made with a stick being dragged across a picket fence (see fig. 45.1). If the stick moves slowly and consistently across the slats, the "trrrr" sound reveals that each "note" sounds clearly and evenly, making them sound fast and clean. If, on the other hand, the stick goes across the slats too fast, it skips over some boards, resulting in notes that will sound unclear and uneven.

Figure 45.1

When practicing scales and technical passages, work with a metronome, initially set at a slow tempo, making sure each single note is played at its full and correct value. Increase the tempo in very small increments, imagining the stick on the fence being dragged steadily and landing in between each board evenly. This takes patience and discipline, but the payoff is a crisp, clear, and mature technique.

SECRET 46: WORKING WITH A PRACTICE PARTNER

Growing up with a twin sister who is also a clarinetist taught me how invaluable a regular practice partner can be. Rather than competing with peers, why not create an atmosphere where everyone grows musically, and therefore, further the art of clarinetistry as a team?

Obviously, one way to work with a practice partner is playing challenging duets, but there are other ways to learn from one another's skills that can be extremely beneficial for both players.

The secret is to find a practice partner who has not only attained a similar level technically and musically, but who has particular instrumental capabilities that you would like to achieve yourself. Similarly, your practice partner will look for the same qualities in you. For example, a strong sight-reader could read advanced etudes with you while you could work on fast tonguing exercises with your practice partner afterward. Either way, both players grow from the experience and can continue to improve at the following joint practice session.

This implies that you choose a practice partner who is not only ready to share the experience but who will also make a significant time commitment so that you both progress steadily. Choose a peer who has a similar schedule that allows you to practice together at a convenient time each week. You may elect to meet every other day or only once a week, and occasionally, you might also want to practice with a different person in order to work on a specific technical problem. One advantage of practicing with different musicians is that it allows your "comfort zone" to fluctuate. This allows you to discover your personal strengths and weaknesses in different contexts and enables you to realize which musical or technical areas need immediate attention.

Once you've found a suitable practice partner, start by warming up separately, and then choose an etude book that is new to both of you. Sight-read each etude together in unison, and try reading the etude with as few stops as possible. If either performer hesitates, encourage getting back on track by continuing to play, or if you find yourself lost, let your partner continue until you find your place. Of course, both players can be flexible and may choose to stop together for a "second try," or to perfect one particularly difficult passage.

Another good way to make use of this time is to practice intonation after both players are warmed up. If both clarinetists have worked on Secret 13: Practicing with the Drone, you should understand good intonation and play in tune with each other. Practice your intonation flexibility by having one player play a slow melody purposely "out of tune" and see if the other can immediately adjust to each questionable pitch, then reverse roles.

Practice partners can also improve their scales together. Practice all key signatures and vary the scales by playing different patterns and rhythms together in unison. Start slowly and increase the tempo at each practice session. You can vary this further by playing scales a third apart.

Fast tonguing is an ideal technique to practice together because it is a measurable skill. Choose a fast staccato etude and turn on the metronome at a comfortable speed. Gradually increase the tempo, and write down the maximum tempo that was achieved on that day, keeping in mind the progress to be made next time. In this setting, both players will naturally be motivated to improve this skill and reach their potential sooner. The teamwork inspires you to persevere and continue playing rather than giving up, as one might be tempted to do when alone in the practice room.

Undoubtedly, independent work in the practice room is of utmost importance. However, working with a peer is an effective technique to enhance individual practice, and it allows skills to be tested outside our usual comfort level.

SECRET 47: PREDICTING MENTAL CONCENTRATION

Often, we find ourselves feeling completely ready to perform a piece of music after hours of practice and preparation. So, why is it that once it is time to perform onstage, a passage might not come out exactly as it did in the practice room? The same could be said for all types of situations, such as lessons, recording sessions, or rehearsals.

The difference is the number of ears actually listening to us. Lone musicians in a practice space are heard by their own two ears. Ideally, in this setting, mental concentration should be at a near maximum. Mental concentration should be focused, deliberate, and thorough, even though the performer's mind may well be too busy for a perfectly accurate self-evaluation.

Once another person enters the practice room, two people are now listening to the performer. The performer might become distracted by this new presence in the room. It is almost as if concentration is cut in half. Add a third person in the room, and one might theorize that concentration is affected even more. When playing in front of an audience of hundreds of people, one's concentration might be reduced to a fraction in terms of effectiveness.

If we pursue this theory, it can be said that potentially, for many of us, the following applies:

1 performer alone = 100% concentration
2 people present = 50% concentration
3 people present = 33% concentration
Full audience = 1% concentration

Therefore, it is necessary to be able to maintain 100 percent concentration in a concert or recording setting to retain focus in times of stress, pressure, or distraction.

If one prepares the material far beyond the usually accepted level, there is more of a guarantee that the live performance will match the accuracy seen in the practice room. Of course, many performers play their best in a concert setting, with adrenaline flowing and the audience's energy bouncing back at them, making the experience much more exciting and successful.

For many clarinetists, however, clever practice strategies can assure them of more secure results. A good technique is to use a recording device to record and review the recently played material, much as if an outside listener came in the room during practice time. After all, what better motivating tool is there than our own highly discerning and critical ears?

Intelligent practice involves understanding a particular passage and repeating it to increase the odds of flawless execution. Even if the material is completely mastered and ready for performance, one should mentally "go back to the drawing board" and continue investigating ways to perfect the execution of the music.

A useful technique to increase mental concentration is to imagine that you are recording the material for a prestigious recording label, and that you only have one chance (or one "take") for each passage. This manner of thinking naturally encourages concentration in a much more focused way, and reminds us that careful mental preparation before playing a single note enhances the final result.

Another idea is to mentally prepare for the performance by practicing the music in the actual concert hall. Envision the audience, experiment with the room's acoustics, and invite musician friends to sit in on the rehearsal. Remember to breathe adequately before playing. The increased amount of oxygen in the blood supplies nourishment to the brain, which is in turn energized to allow full concentration. Our mathematical theory may conclude as follows:

100% preparation = 50% probability of flawless performance
150% preparation = 75% probability of flawless performance
200% preparation = 99% probability of flawless performance

And for the brave:

225% preparation = The best press review yet!

SECRET 48: SIGHT-READING

Just as a jazz artist needs to master improvisation—the ability to perform spontaneously without the aid of manuscript or memory—so does a classical musician need skill in sight-reading, which is the ability to read music without preparation. Both skills demand confidence, proper training, memory, and theoretical understanding.

Many performers worry about playing the correct notes instead of concentrating on rhythm. Because music usually involves coordinating several parts, it is essential to concentrate on proper rhythm first rather than being too concerned about stumbling on a sharp or flat.

Learning sight-reading can be compared to learning how to read books; the more rhythms and patterns you practice (either from method books or repertoire), the better your sight-reading will become over time.

Other components of sight-reading such as tempos, dynamics, articulations, key changes, ornaments, and extreme registers also need to be practiced. These should be worked on only after proper rhythmic accuracy is achieved. The following example illustrates some basic rhythmic problems. Try singing the following binary passage while steadily tapping the tempo:

Figure 48.1

Did you ask yourself how many beats or bars you just sang? I hope not. For the first step of this exercise, simply think of each note or rest independently, and hold each note for its proper value.

In duple meter, there are two eighth notes in one beat. When you tap, notice that you need *two* hand motions for each beat: down and up. Therefore, for one quarter note you need two motions: down-up, or up-down, depending on where the note falls in relation to the beat. Try the following exercise and, while tapping each beat, assign a number for each motion. Say "one-two" for each beat, that is, "one" for an eighth note, "one-two-three" for a dotted quarter, and "one-two-three-four" for a half note. Tap each motion evenly, and associate each number with one movement, either down or up ("D" and "U"), as shown in fig. 48.2.

Now try this same exercise starting on the *up*beat. The sense of the rhythm fitting perfectly within a bar is quite lost, but surely you have made your way easily through the entire phrase.

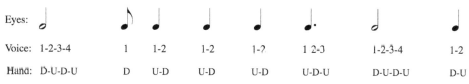

Figure 48.2

For more complicated rhythms, such as in the next exercise, it is necessary to combine reading techniques; when playing triplets in duple meter (or duplets in triple meter), count entire beats *instead* of subdividing. For sixteenth notes, assign two even notes within each motion, three notes for sixteenth triplets, and so on:

Figure 48.3

For ternary rhythms, tap three motions: "down-up-up":

Figure 48.4

The "one-two" or "down-up" method is especially helpful for quickly changing meters such as in Stravinsky's *The Rite of Spring*.

Another crucial aspect of sight-reading is note accuracy. Oddly enough, one of the best ways to improve sight-reading is to develop technical independence *without* sheet music. An experienced performer will be able to analyze and identify technical patterns at sight. For example, an excerpt might be made up of a series of chromatic patterns, followed by a set of arpeggios. The trained musician uses previously memorized exercises and instinctively executes them when they appear on the page.

Practice your own exercises from memory and in all major and minor keys. Include ascending and descending exercises on the chromatic scale (see Secret 51: Developing Technical Independence). While playing these by ear, try to visualize the written notes or, if necessary, write out the beginning of each exercise. At first it may appear quite challenging, but each exercise gets easier as you go along.

Eventually, when you see such passages in your music, you will not need to read the notes in detail; they will simply appear as patterns you have already stored in your memory. I call this type of practice "imagery." Sight-read as much as possible. Learning to read any language requires daily practice, much as we did in grade school when we were learning to read books.

Playing duets is an excellent way to improve sight-reading. Form a duo with a good reader and try to play through the music with as few stops as possible. This will compel your eyes to move ahead.

Rhythmic solfège is a very helpful sight-reading technique taught in French conservatories. Unlike traditional solfège where the notes are sung with their respective pitch names, rhythmic solfège involves naming each note in rhythm while hand-tapping each beat without singing. Use whichever nomenclature you prefer ("do-re-mi" or "A-B-C"), and start with a slow and steady tempo. Name each note correctly without changing the tempo (naming accidentals is not necessary). This exercise is surprisingly tricky. Start very slowly to avoid stumbling; this enables you to virtually x-ray the music and identify each note more effectively. After some practice, challenge yourself and try doing the exercise with another person in unison. In addition to hearing pitches internally before you play them, try to associate note alterations or accidentals with fingerings, much like visualizing a graphic. Viewing passages with many alterations as part of a larger picture will make them easier to execute.

Another great tool is the online virtual accompaniment system, SmartMusic. The program has numerous levels of sight-reading exercises. The music is revealed on the screen and the count-off click begins after the selected amount of study time has elapsed. You can create your own sight-reading exercises and progress through various levels of difficulty.

Along with the ability to sight-read notes, one must also read other musical details at sight such as articulations, rhythm, and dynamics. With the help of these exercises, players will find different ways of making the art of sight-reading an enjoyable challenge rather than a difficult task. May your first readings become the best ones yet.

SECRET 49: TRANSPOSITION

Have you ever found yourself in one of these scenarios? Your band director needs you to cover an oboe part in a piece you are playing but you have no idea why your notes are not fitting in with everyone else. Or you have been asked to play in a musical and you suddenly see *change to flute* and *to saxophone* in your part, but you don't play flute or saxophone and need to play the parts on your clarinet. By the time you figure out how to transpose the parts, the musical is over!

Dr. Shelley Jagow, professor of music, band director and woodwind specialist at Wright State University, offers the following advice (see from here to the end of the Secret):

If you play a C on the piano and then a C on your clarinet, or if you want to play duets with your flute friend, each instrument will produce a different pitch. This may seem very confusing and you may wish that all instruments were pitched in C. However, if we pitched every instrument in C in relation to A=440, we would have to learn a multiple set of fingerings for each instrument. Imagine using one set of fingerings to play B♭ clarinet, and a different set of fingerings to play A clarinet. This would be cumbersome and impractical.

In order to have an ensemble full of rich colors of varying timbres and registers, instruments have been built in different keys. The clarinet is a "transposing" instrument, while other wind instruments in C (flute, oboe, bassoon) are "nontransposing" instruments. The main clarinets are pitched in B♭, A, and E♭. If each clarinet were to play their written C, it would sound as a different note or octave than each other. Figure 49.1 shows the actual note that would be sounding on each clarinet. So how do clarinetists transpose the music of another instrument?

Clarinet	Transpose	Written	Play
E♭ Clarinet	UP minor 3rd (3 half-steps)		
B♭ Clarinet	DOWN Major 2nd (2 half-steps)		
A Clarinet	DOWN minor 3rd (3 half-steps)		

Figure 49.1

Option 1: Write Out the Transposition

Obtain the music in advance so you have the time to rewrite the part by hand, or you can use a multitude of notation programs to digitally transpose the part to a new key. In order to correctly rewrite the part to sound at the same pitch, you will need to transpose as indicated in fig. 49.2.

B♭ Clarinet (If you are asked to play this part)		Transpose the written notes AND the key signature	Written	You play
Flute Oboe	Pitched in C	Read the part **UP M2** since the B♭ Clarinet sounds a M2 lower than these C-pitched instruments.  = M2	 o	 o (Add 2♯)
Soprano Saxophone Trumpet	Pitched in B♭	Yay! The clarinet is also pitched in B♭ so you do not need to transpose anything.	 o	 o
A Clarinet	Pitched in A	Read the part **DOWN m2** since the B♭ Clarinet sounds a half-step higher than A Clarinet.  = m2	 o	 o (Add 5♯)
English Horn Horn	Pitched in F	Read the part **DOWN P4** since the B♭ Clarinet sounds a Perfect 4th higher than these F-pitched instruments  = P4	 o	 o (Add 1♯)
Alto Clarinet Alto Saxophone	Pitched in E♭	Read the part **DOWN P5** since the B♭ Clarinet sounds a Perfect 5th higher than these E♭-pitched instruments  = P5	 o	 o (Add 1♭)

Figure 49.2

Option 2: Play the Transposition at Sight

This is less time-consuming than writing out a new part, but does take some practice. First, you need to know the key of the instrument, and then you can transpose to *sound* the same pitch as the instrument part. For example, if you need to play a flute part, first know that the key of flute is pitched in C; then you must transpose the flute part UP an M2 (Major second). For an F on flute, you need to play a G. The G on your clarinet will *sound* the same as a flute playing the F. Remember to also transpose the key signature. For example, if the flute part is in the key of B♭, then transpose the key UP an M2 in order to read the part in the key of C. Be careful of accidentals:

If you need to *raise* a natural, then it will be a sharp.
If you need to *raise* a sharp, then it will be a double-sharp.
If you need to *lower* a flat, then it will be a double-flat.

SECRET 50: UNUSUAL TRANSPOSITIONS IN ORCHESTRAL EXCERPTS

Orchestral clarinetists usually choose to transpose "C clarinet" parts on the B♭ clarinet. There are some cases, however, where using either a C (if available) or A clarinet instead of B♭ might prove more practical. Here is a selected list of orchestral excerpts *in C*, usually played on the B♭ clarinet, with suggested transpositions.

- Beethoven's Concerto for Violin (3rd mvt, Larghetto): Use A clarinet, since all other movements are written for A clarinet.
- Brahms's Symphony No. 4 (3rd mvt, Allegro giocoso): The A may be used since all other movements are written for A clarinet.
- Mahler's Symphony No. 2 (2nd mvt, Andante con moto): The section in C has five sharps. Transposing on A instead of B♭ clarinet is simpler.
- Smetana's Overture to the opera *The Bartered Bride*: The *Vivacissimo* staccato passage is more idiomatic on the C clarinet (if you can locate a C instrument).

Other transpositions may be considered, such as A clarinet excerpts played on B♭, or E♭ clarinet excerpts played on D clarinet, and vice versa (again, if you can locate a D clarinet):

- Borodin's *Polovetsian Dances* from *Prince Igor*: Although the Andantino solo is ideal on A clarinet, it is quite short and there is not much time to change back to the B♭ clarinet for the very important technical solo in the following Allegro vivo. I suggest playing the Andantino solo on B♭ instead of A.
- Brahms's Symphony No. 1: The Andante is best played on B♭ instead of A for two reasons: the cumbersome high c♯² becomes a smooth c², and the remainder of the symphony is on B♭ clarinet.
- Dvořák's *New World Symphony No. 9*, op. 95: The entire piece is on A clarinet, except for bars 11–26 (mvt 2), which are on B♭ clarinet. For convenience, transpose bars 11–26 on A clarinet.
- Debussy's *Afternoon of a Faun*: It is convenient to play the last section of the A clarinet excerpt on B♭ so the instrument will already be warmed up for the following exposed solo on B♭ clarinet (at rehearsal number 6).
- Shostakovitch's Symphony No. 5: The third movement, Largo, sounds smoother on B♭ clarinet. The original part in A contains many awkward sharps.
- Berlioz's *Symphonie fantastique* (5th mvt, "A Witches' Sabbath"): The first clarinetist should also prepare the second clarinet solo part in case the second clarinetist is assigned to play the E♭ clarinet solo from the first part, or if the second clarinetist cannot play the performance. Also, both performers

might want to bring an E♭ instrument in case of emergency part-switching. Normally, the first clarinet plays the E♭ solo, since it is written on the first clarinet part. The fifth movement's second clarinet part is in C and should be played on B♭ clarinet.

- Bizet's *Carmen, Act II Entr'acte*: The B♭ clarinet clarion trill (f♯^{1}–g♯^{1}) is much easier on A, unless a (relatively rare) B♭ clarinet equipped with a special articulated g♯^{1} key is used.
- Ginastera's *Variations Concertantes*: The B♭ clarinet variation is more idiomatic on A, except for the altississimo d^3 at the end of the variation.
- Strauss, R., *Till Eulenspiegel*: The piccolo clarinet part is originally for the (relatively rare) D clarinet. Handwritten, transposed parts for E♭ clarinet were floating around orchestral libraries for years until Peter Hadcock published the part in E♭ in his book *Orchestral Studies for the E♭ Clarinet* (Roncorp).
- Ravel's *Daphnis et Chloé*, Suite No. 2: For D clarinet owners, some sections in the E♭ clarinet part can be played more smoothly on D clarinet (if you can locate an instrument), especially during sections with a five-sharp key signature.

SECRET 51: DEVELOPING TECHNICAL INDEPENDENCE

The clarinet is an instrument capable of amazing technical prowess, and composers of yesterday and today certainly took advantage of this when creating our repertoire. A vast number of exercise and etude books are available to help improve finger technique; however, I believe it is important not only to develop technical *ability*, but technical *independence* as well. Technical independence (playing without music) allows us to become better sight-readers and more flexible musicians.

One way to become less dependent on the notes on the page is to memorize crucial technical patterns found in our basic repertoire. These include all kinds of ascending and descending patterns based on the chromatic scale, such as chromatic minor seconds, thirds, chromatic perfect fourths and fifths, and so on. The following exercises are written out in part, and should be eventually memorized so they can easily be used as daily warm-up routines. Octaves are important to master, as our instrument does not have an octave key and utilizes dramatically different fingerings from one octave to another. Various articulations should be applied, with various interval combinations. Major, minor, diminished, and augmented arpeggios may also be transposed. Simply write down a very short musical pattern and transpose it chromatically. Figures 51.1 and 51.2 are some examples.

Figure 51.1

Figure 51.2

SECRET 52: ALTISSIMO CHROMATIC FINGERINGS

Clarinetists enjoy the luxury of being able to choose from different fingerings for each note, especially in the altissimo register. There are closed fingerings that yield a powerful tone, and there are open fingerings that can be valuable technical shortcuts. Tom Ridenour's *Altissimo Register* is an excellent book that contains a wide variety of altissimo fingering options. Ridenour describes contexts in which to use various fingerings and even includes blank fingering charts for users to fill out on their own. I find that the fingering chart in fig. 52.1 offers a very simple way to play chromatically, from altissimo A to C.

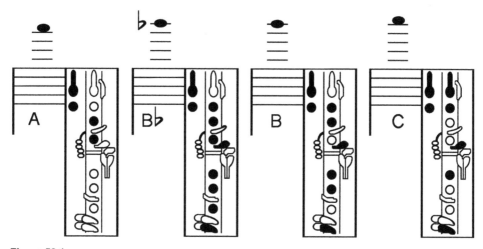

Figure 52.1

The pattern is easy to remember and results in effective response. Here is an easy way to memorize the fingerings:

1. Note that the altissimo A has no A♭/e♭ key.
2. Altissimo B♭ is like a c¹ (third space on the staff) with a left little finger G♯ key.
3. Altissimo B is the previous B♭ fingering minus both ring fingers.
4. Altissimo C is the previous B fingering minus both middle fingers plus the "throat a" key to correct flatness.

SECRET 53: ALTISSIMO REGISTER RESPONSE

Advanced clarinetists who are ready to tackle the altissimo register may find it difficult to make the notes speak on a consistent basis. Oftentimes, the idea of playing altissimo translates into biting on the reed, choking off reed vibration that results in a thin and brittle sound, or no sound at all. Instead of biting the reed and closing your jaw, move your jaw forward (as if it were a desk drawer being opened) in small increments, depending on the note's pitch. Keep your top teeth in a fixed position near the mouthpiece tip, without sliding the mouthpiece further into the mouth. Imagine a miniature set of stairs on the reed where each step corresponds to a specific pitch. The jaw moves forward almost creating an underbite, and as the notes go higher, slightly move the jaw lower on the reed while maintaining the forward position.

Figure 53.1 illustrates the various jaw positions and their corresponding pitches. The "x" represents the point at which the teeth underneath the lower lip should apply pressure on each line.

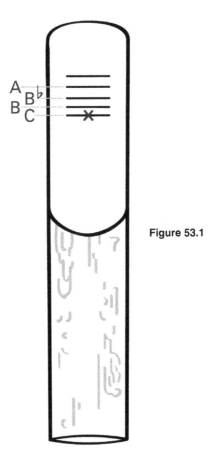

Figure 53.1

SECRET 54: SUPER ALTISSISSIMO REGISTER

Altissimo is usually the highest register played by advanced clarinetists. Composers are now requesting super altississimo register, which was previously uncharted. Super altississimo virtuoso Robert Spring, professor of clarinet at Arizona State University, offers the following advice on achieving notes higher than c^3, going up to f^3:

Until the last two or three decades, written notes for the soprano clarinet rarely went higher than altissimo a^3. There might have been a few exceptions; however, they were rare. In the 1960s and early 1970s, composers experimented with ultra-high notes, but this was often notated "teeth on reed" to achieve pitches. These were seldom accurate and in tune, but used mostly for effect. Composers eventually began writing actual pitches, and it was up to the performer to "invent" a fingering to make these happen. Today's composers are routinely writing up to super altississimo e^3.

The soft tissue in the oral cavity changes for virtually every pitch we play, therefore the performer needs to train the oral cavity and learn to control those muscles, much like saxophonists who practice harmonics to perfect their altissimo register.

Begin by playing an open g, and overblowing to altissimo d^2 without using the register key. This can be challenging at first. An easier approach is to slur from clarion g^1 to an "open" d^2 and then voice down to get the open g. Doing this several times will help establish the changes in the oral cavity necessary to begin producing the super altissimo range.

Next, work your way down the chalumeau register; f♯ to c♯, f to c, and then down to c to g. It is crucial to do this *without* using the register key. Finally, practice playing an entire C major scale in the clarion register without using the register key. This is very challenging, and the performer will always get a few grunts in the notes, but it will provide the "feel" necessary to begin working in this extreme register.

The next step is reviewing the fingerings that you use to comfortably perform a chromatic scale from clarion c^2 to altissimo c^3. (There are many fingering possibilities, such as in Secret 52: Altissimo Chromatic Fingerings.) My preferred fingering for altissimo c^3 is illustrated in fig. 54.1.

To get into the next register, most performers will initially need to articulate each note (see the fingerings). The performer is urged to invent other fingerings if necessary. Changing the keys played by the little fingers can help get the desired note to sound.

I had to literally invent these fingerings for several pieces I was learning, most notably for my *Tarantella* recording that includes violin repertoire. The main issue is that when a composer realizes that these high notes can be played, they write them and then we need to perform them! Some composers write as high as e^3.

The key is to be patient. Learning the super altississimo register can take several months, but once the correct throat movement technique is achieved, these notes will become a part of your musical sound palette.

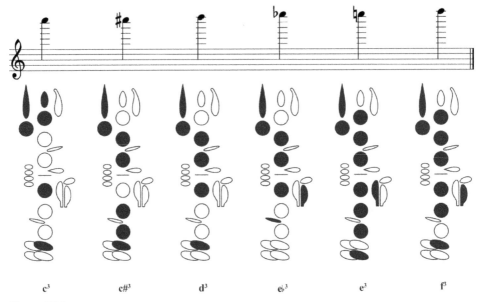

Figure 54.1

SECRET 55: PRACTICING IN FRONT OF A MIRROR OR VIDEO CAMERA

Practicing in front of a mirror or a video camera is an excellent way to check on various technical aspects of your playing such as embouchure, finger position, body movement, and posture. It is also a good way to detect body tension during playing.

Mirror

Music stand mirrors are available at some music stores, or you can purchase a "locker" mirror with a magnet on the back and attach it to your music stand. Better yet, install a large mirror on your practice room wall. To begin, play passages you have memorized so you can concentrate on playing without looking at your music. Some of the things to look for are finger height and evenness, flat chin embouchure, the amount of reed and mouthpiece in the mouth, the instrument's angle while playing, inadvertent raising of shoulders, foot tapping on the floor, and posture.

Naturally, everything you will see will be a mirror image so it can be a bit confusing at first. The good news is that focusing on your mirror image increases your self-awareness, which is a great way to prepare for a live performance because it takes you away from your zone of concentration, just as would occur in front of an audience. Moreover, using a mirror is practical, efficient, and inexpensive. Verify what you have learned with your private teacher to see if you are interpreting your observations correctly. You may be surprised at what you discover while practicing this way.

Video Camera

Using a video camera, computer, or smartphone is even better than using a mirror because you can replay video clips when you are finished playing and can assess each movement without any distractions from playing.

Position your device in such a way that you can clearly view what you are trying to capture. Review the clips in slow motion to evaluate various techniques and save the files to document your progress or to share with your teacher later on. If you are recording a rehearsal with an accompanist, save the good takes for your website or for audition and portfolio materials. These techniques are a great way to increase your rate of progression because you are being proactive and acting as your own teacher between lessons.

QUICK-TIPS BULLETIN BOARD—TECHNIQUE

- Practice makes perfect. Imagine the serial number on the clarinet joint as an odometer to remind you to keep adding hours to your "practice mileage."
- Although good finger position requires that your fingers be relatively close to the keys and rings, all bets are off for trills. Lift your finger high when playing a trill to allow both notes to be equal in importance. Keeping the finger too close to the key or tone hole tends to make the lower note sound more important or longer than the upper note. Each note in a trill should sound equal in tone and length.
- Do not collapse or "cave in" your fingers as you play. Check in the mirror for gently curved fingers.
- Trim your fingernails on your little fingers, to prevent slipping on the keys.
- Pick random spots in your piece to see if you can play any section out of context.
- Work like a slingshot: Take a few steps back and practice at slower tempos so you can propel your progress forward later on.
- Compare scales to street maps: If you know where you are going, you will make the correct turns in time. If not, you will get lost. Visualize and memorize the feel of an entire scale pattern before playing it to minimize the risk of errors.
- Practice the chromatic scale, starting and ending with E on the left as well as E on the right. This will create two different patterns, which are equal in importance.
- Always remember to play the high register $c^2\#$ (two lines above the staff) with no right little finger on the $A\flat/e\flat^1$ key, as this will keep you from being sharp on the $c\#^2$. Use the $A\flat/e\flat^1$ key for all notes above $c^2\#$ for correct intonation and more ring in the tone.

CHAPTER 5

Musicianship Strategies

SECRET 56: REMEMBERING NATURE

Nature's forces are around us every day. The wind blows gently on a mild sunny day, but it roars intensely during a storm. Waves predictably crash on the seashore, birds take flight, and the laws of gravity and nature prevail.

I find it helpful to remember nature when playing a musical phrase. Contrasting forces of nature result in numerous kinds of energy levels; the impetus (the energy associated with movement) of an ascending scale is different compared to a descending scale, high and low notes have contrasting and unique expressive traits, and long and short notes possess opposite characteristics.

Playing an ascending scale can be compared to a person running up a hill, whereas a descending scale can be visualized as running down the same hill. Running uphill requires momentum that gradually dissipates. Running down a hill results in acceleration until the bottom is reached. A similar image would be the action of throwing an object up in the air compared to the motion of the object falling down.

Similar ideas can be applied to musical phrasing. A singer is closest to nature because the body acts as a musical instrument. The singer executing a large ascending interval will naturally face different physical challenges than when singing a large descending interval. An instrumentalist gains by imitating nature in order to play with as much human personality as possible, rather than taking a more mechanical and technical approach when interpreting a musical phrase. When playing an ascending passage, one can borrow nature's principles and increase the "intent" (or air speed) with a crescendo, much like running up a hill. In contrast, a descending passage can start gently, as if on top of a roller coaster track, and then glides down with a slight crescendo until the phrase naturally decreases dynamically. Needless to say, however, tempo markings must be observed, and there should be no unintended rushing or slowing down. Written dynamics should also be observed, but always keep in mind the forces of nature that help guide those dynamics.

Of course, one must consider the context of a phrase and the instrument's registers and capabilities before making a musical decision. A sustained tone has less impact when sitting still. Instead, it can be compared to the continuous moving force of the blowing wind; the long tone travels forward with varying air speeds and tone colors appropriate with the musical phrase direction, resulting in a more expressive interpretation.

When playing an accelerando passage, it is important to realize how acceleration works in nature. For instance, an animal can only reach maximum running speed after a period of acceleration (the same is true with a car, for that matter). Realizing this can encourage the player not to accelerate in an uneven, forced, and artificial way. Sometimes I am asked, "How do you come up with all this?" My reply is always the same: I don't come up with it, because it is already there. I simply borrow nature's powers and copy her every chance I get.

There are so many examples that can be drawn from nature to inspire a most convincing interpretation. After all, isn't Nature herself a masterpiece worthy of perpetual and continuous imitation?

SECRET 57: MEMORIZATION

Memorizing your music is a great way to know it thoroughly and communicate it to your audience without any barriers. Whether you are memorizing a concerto for a competition or memorizing a marching band show, the benefits of playing without music are worth the extra time and effort in the practice room. On the other hand, performing with music can reduce anxiety. Also, if the performer is not quite ready to perform by memory, the experience can be distressing and also become an uneasy distraction for the audience. The following advice is intended for performers whose goal is to perform by memory.

Before memorizing a classical piece, make sure to start learning it correctly by using the music. Pay close attention to tempos, dynamics, and articulation. In the case of popular, jazz, folk, or world music, it depends on the individual, but I suggest learning it by ear at first, and then tweaking details with the sheet music later (if available).

Memorizing a piece of music alone in a practice room is one thing; however, memorizing a piece along with the accompaniment is much better in the long run. If you practice the clarinet line by yourself, chances are that once the accompaniment is present, you will be out of your comfort zone and might be surprised at how little information remains in your memory, even after hours of work. I suggest four strategies to memorize music with accompaniment:

1. Ask an accompanist to work with you early on during your memorization process.
2. Work with the virtual accompaniment system SmartMusic. Not only will the virtual piano accompaniment follow your tempo changes, but it can play the solo line along with you, play in any tempo, and repeat passages as many times as necessary.
3. When you are ready to play at the performance tempo, rehearse with accompaniment with the music, and then without the music.
4. Once you have successfully played your entire memorized piece several times over the course of a few weeks, invite friends to listen to you. Having an audience is a good way to simulate the distractions that occur on the concert stage.

It is important to plan *how* you will memorize your music. If you do not begin the process soon enough, you may be pressed for time to learn the end of your piece and, as a result, be less certain of those sections compared to the beginning sections. Decide on a number of bars to be learned each day and increase the number daily. Here is an example of a plan:

1. Memorize four bars on the first day. Analyze and understand the material theoretically, musically, and by ear. Continue your practice routine with your other material.
2. The next day, play the four bars you learned and add four more. Again, analyze and understand the material and continue with your daily practice routine.
3. The third day, add yet another four bars. At first, it may be tedious to memorize music, but you will notice an increase in your efficiency as you gain experience.
4. Be sure to arm yourself with a lot of patience, especially when learning long pieces from the classical and romantic periods.

Memorizing music is challenging work, but the process will undoubtedly help you grow as a musician and convey your musical message more convincingly.

SECRET 58: LISTENING TO OPERA ARIAS

A great way to expand your musical horizons as an instrumentalist is to listen to opera arias. An understanding of the singing voice can transform an instrumentalist into a lyricist, and therefore, drastically increase musical expression and tonal color.

Because the human voice is an integral part of the body, with characteristics dictated by nature, biology, and physiology, the voice perfectly illustrates how musical phrases are naturally interpreted. Discerning instrumentalists can learn a great deal from the voice's natural beauty of expression by paying attention to minute details such as how great singers perform ascending and descending intervals, dynamic contrasts, and tonal colors. Similarly, instrumentalists who understand the operatic genre can shift from instrumental to vocal styles (and vice versa) within the same piece of music. The four important elements of an opera are as follows:

1. Aria (song relating to the opera's story)
2. Recitative (spoken material between arias that helps move the story along)
3. Instrumental section (overture or instrumental section between scenes and at the end of the opera)
4. Vocalise (cadenza-like section sung on one or more vowels within an aria)

By observing subtle variations in dynamics and tonal color in ascending and descending passages within arias and vocalises, instrumentalists can more easily understand the natural flow of a phrase in instrumental cadenzas. A great way to learn the many facets of opera is to see onstage productions either live or on video. Observing singers breathing with a correct posture and studying how their bodies move with the music adds another dimension to an instrumentalist's point of view.

A good understanding of these four elements can significantly improve the performance of operatic-style clarinet repertoire such as Weber's concertos, Rossini's *Introduction, Theme and Variations*, various opera fantasies by Verdi, arranged by Bassi and Loverglio, and etudes such as Cavallini's *30 Caprices*. By differentiating between technical (such as orchestral interludes) and lyrical (such as arias) sections, instrumentalists can add tremendous breadth and expression to their performances.

To begin, I suggest listening the very well-known aria "E lucevan le stelle" ("And the stars were shining") from Puccini's opera *Tosca*. It is from the third act and is sung by Tosca's love (tenor) while he is languishing in his doomed fate as a prisoner. This aria is a perfect example because it is preceded by an exquisite clarinet solo with the same melody. My favorite version is sung by the late Salvatore Licitra, on his recording entitled *The Debut*.

While listening to the tenor, notice the subtle gliding of the voice between ascending and descending intervals. Since the clarinet cannot precisely replicate this effect, subtle color changes in the tone can be used instead. For example, when playing a descending interval in an *ff*, end the first note with a sudden drop in dynamic (*ff* going to *pp*) immediately before playing the lower note. Think of the magical moment on top of a roller coaster where time stands still before the descent. This weightless sensation is exactly like the drop in dynamic of the voice gliding down from the top note to the low note.

Another voice trait that can be emulated is that of human emotion. While playing a crescendo, you might intensify the note not only by increasing the dynamic level, but also increasing its harmonic content. This can be accomplished by gradually adding harmonics to your sound as you crescendo (playing with increasingly dark and intense overtones with faster airflow), and conversely removing harmonics (or playing with a lighter tone) during decrescendos.

It is important to remember that even though instrumentalists do not use language or diction to express a musical phrase, they do use articulation. Just as the spoken voice enunciates words using vowels and consonants, instruments such as the clarinet imitate vowels and consonants by slurring or tonguing notes. Inaccurate articulation results in an inconsistent and unclear musical phrase. Pay close attention to all details in your music and adhere to the notated articulation as intended by the composer.

Additionally, it is fascinating to study details such as facial makeup worn by opera singers. The makeup emphasizes facial features, which is essential for the audience to notice accurate facial expressions from considerable distances. A similar approach is necessary so that words sung can be clearly understood by the audience. For this to be possible, singers (as well as actors) need to exaggerate enunciation and emotion in order to convey the intended message across the entire hall. Instrumentalists can apply the same principle and envision they are speaking and projecting a clear message through their instruments. Listening to great opera arias can significantly transform your perception of phrasing and open up a whole new world of musical expression. You will be pleased to hear the subtleties in your tonal color and musical line once you develop and apply these concepts. Observing the singers' array of facial expressions paired with spectacular costumes and scenery completes the equation.

SECRET 59: PLAYING WITH PIANO ACCOMPANIMENT

To create the best overall musical effect, it is important for the clarinetist to understand and complement the piano accompaniment. When playing a sonata with piano, for example, it is imperative to view the musical content as an equal duet as opposed to playing a solo with background accompaniment. Here are some ideas to consider while playing with piano:

1. Notice when the clarinet and piano exchange identical or similar musical phrases and make them dovetail into one another flawlessly, instead of playing separate sections, glued together and disjointed. You might think of this as smoothly "passing the relay race stick" from one line to the other rather than taking turns at a passage.

2. When the clarinet ends a phrase with a long note, notice if the piano plays a moving line so you can complement the line instead of simply playing the long note for the correct number of beats. For example, if the piano plays an ascending scale or a crescendo, try to mesh your long note with the piano line by imitating the dynamic direction and tonal contrasts, and by complementing the chord progressions.

3. Be sure to end long notes at the correct moment so they won't interfere with the piano's next phrase.

4. Practice with piano often so that your intonation will be as accurate as possible. Remember that a piano that is tuned correctly will play intervals without variation, while wind instruments' intonation can vary on each note depending on technique, embouchure, air support, and room temperature. Practicing with the online interactive accompaniment system SmartMusic® is a handy way to prepare for rehearsals with piano.

5. It is important to choose a pianist who understands the art of playing within a duo (or chamber ensemble) rather than as a soloist. A chamber music piano sound and style differ significantly from a concerto soloist's approach. Both have merits, but an accompanist will know to complement the instrumentalist during various sections, depending on the prominence of the clarinet's part in the score at any given moment.

6. Although the clarinet and the piano have drastically different tones, it is essential to be able to match in tonal color when playing together. Listen to your favorite clarinet and piano recordings, and note how both parts mesh together.

7. The piano is a very rich-sounding instrument because of its huge resonance chamber (wood shell), so the sound continues to ring after the playing has stopped. In contrast, the clarinet has a very small resonance chamber (cylindrical tube) and does not resonate after the air stops. To complement the piano's resonance, taper the ends of your notes with an almost inaudible decrescendo rather than abruptly stopping the sound.

SECRET 60: PREPARING YOUR MUSIC BEFORE THE PERFORMANCE

Your sheet music will never fall off your stand except on the very hour of your concert.

—Murphy's Law

One should not underestimate the importance of preparing sheet music before a performance. Dropping a loose sheet of music in the middle of an exposed part is a sure way to make it fall flat, literally. Here are simple ways to prepare music parts:

1. If more than two pages need to be placed together on a music stand, secure pages together from top to bottom with adhesive tape so they will remain in the proper order and stay flat on the stand.
2. Carefully plan your music so that page turns are efficient and practical. This might mean rearranging certain pages or cutting them horizontally in two (the binding will hold the separated sections together) so that the top part can be turned first and the bottom part later during a rest.
3. If the music consists of a collection of loose sheets, clearly number each one so that the order is correct every time.
4. If you change the order of movements for any reason, clearly note this in your music so that you will not forget during the performance. Performance anxiety can result in surprising memory slips, so it is better to be safe than sorry.
5. Clearly mark your music with special dynamics or tempo changes. This saves time during practice and also helps you to recall the smallest details during performances. You may choose to write in pencil or a color pencil or highlighter for crucial information; however, only light pencil markings should be made on rental or borrowed parts, and these should be erased before returning them.
6. If you wish to play a piece without turning pages, consider reducing its size by cutting all margins and attaching the pages together so that they will all fit together on the stand. If reduction is not practical, plan to use two stands and practice with both stands beforehand. Note that photocopying published music is illegal.
7. Do not wait until the last minute to plan your sheet music setup, as tricky page turns need to be practiced ahead of time.
8. If an extra page needs to be unfolded from the part before the performance, mark "unfold page" at the very top of your first page.
9. When marking chamber music parts, refrain from writing colleagues' names as cues ("Mike" or "Angie"), as chamber music personnel changes on a regular basis. Instead, write the instrument's cue, such as "oboe cue." Planning ahead can make the difference between a successful performance and a disappointing one. As the Girl and Boy Scouts say: *Be prepared!*

SECRET 61: KEEP A PRACTICE JOURNAL

A journal is a very efficient way to keep track of one's progress in the practice room. It can be surprising how quickly important details can be forgotten, and how making note of daily improvements can be a great motivator for reaching goals. Journals can be useful for all kinds of other endeavors as well. For example, some bodybuilders maintain their motivation by keeping track of their exercise routine in a journal and by creating video blogs of their gradual physical transformations.

Here are some suggestions for how to keep a journal to maximize the effectiveness of your daily practice:

1. If you are taking lessons, find a quiet spot immediately after each session and take a moment to list the ideas you found most helpful. This way, you will remember the new concepts to work on without interrupting the lesson to take notes.

2. If you have a particular problem (tonguing, for example), list various corrective methods you used and, after a few days, make note of those that work best. This will also help you design your pedagogy later on if you enter the teaching profession.

3. Find ways to measure your progress quantitatively. For example, keep track of metronome tempos attained for certain exercises and use this information as a basis of comparison for future results. You can do the same for tonguing and technical progress, the timing of your long tones (measured in seconds), and so on.

4. Draw graphics to illustrate certain points. For example, draw the embouchure concepts you learned to clarify your own perception, and as mentioned previously, to help develop your pedagogical skills as a future teacher.

5. Write down how you practice and keep a schedule to make sure you use your time as efficiently as possible. For example, list elements included in your practice. These items could include the following:
   • Warm up body (arms, hands, wrists, neck, and shoulders)
   • Ten minutes of long tones
   • Ten minutes of scales
   • Fifteen minutes of etudes
   • Five-minute break (to avoid tendon injuries)
   • Thirty minutes of solo repertoire
   • Fifteen minutes of orchestral, band, or chamber music excerpts
   The preceding items amount to about one and one-half hours of practice material and, naturally, the list will vary depending on individual situations.

6. List items to be learned or improved upon in the future and check off each item as you achieve it. This helps monitor your progress and gives you a

sense of accomplishment as you go down the list, not to mention that it will prevent you from overlooking important points. Some items might include increasing tempos of specific technical passages each day or the number of bars you were able to memorize. Writing down observations will help you become more aware of details and improve practice efficiency later on.

7. Write questions to ask your teacher during your next lesson. Mark your music and refer to related questions in your journal. It is easy to forget important questions, so bring your journal to your lesson, and ask away.

These are only a few suggestions. You will undoubtedly come up with your own ideas as you progress. The main objective is to make sure you dedicate a special notebook for this and not dilute it with other subjects. If preferred, a binder can be used so that pages can be removed or moved around if needed. Later on, you will appreciate having saved the information, especially if you become a professional performer or teacher.

Practice Journal Apps

While notebooks are a handy way to keep a journal, practice journal apps offer much more. You can quickly enter your information and automatically log practice time, use the built-in metronome that remembers the last speed you practiced, export summary reports, track your progress, organize and label your repertoire, and share your data.

You may also try trading journal notes with a peer to compare experiences and exchange practice strategies, and you may even wish to blog some of your entries.

SECRET 62: PRACTICE TACTICS

The idea of "practice makes perfect" sounds logical in theory but can often be disregarded on a daily basis. Professionals know that seemingly endless hours of rigorous practice are the key to high-level success for aspiring clarinetists. There are so many distractions, excuses, and reasons not to practice. Texting, social media, gaming, and countless leisure activities compete for our attention. In his book *The Outliers: The Story of Success*, author Malcolm Gladwell states that researchers have found that it takes about ten thousand hours for the brain to assimilate what it needs to know to achieve true mastery in a discipline. For clarinetists, success might mean reaching the level of proficiency required to seriously compete in auditions for professional positions.

Sergeant Diane Gingras, clarinetist with the Central Band of the Canadian Armed Forces, (and my twin sister), offers several practice tactics (see from here to the end of the Secret):

Tactic 1: How Much Practice Is Necessary?

Let's do the math. Our aspiring professional musician is a fifteen-year-old student who takes clarinet lessons and practices four hours a day. By the age of twenty-one, this individual will have logged 7,200 hours of practice (subtract sixty days a year for the inevitable time away from practice). That is remarkable, but probably not sufficient to reach maximum potential. When you sit in an ensemble, you will invariably find people who can tackle difficult passages more effectively than others. They are the ones who have mastered double tonguing or know the special fingerings that allow them to breeze through the music. Diligent practice enables you to master advanced skills that will make it possible to play virtually any part, so let's do the math again. Our would-be professional musician begins a serious practice regimen one year earlier, at fourteen years of age, takes lessons, attends music camps during three or four summers, majors in music in college, and practices five hours a day until the age of twenty-one. This routine yields approximately 10,500 hours of practice time and performance experience, which should be sufficient preparation to compete effectively in the professional arena as a young adult.

Tactic 2: The Payoff

When you encounter an extremely fast staccato passage, such as *Italian in Algiers* by Rossini, do you have the skills necessary to play detached sixteenth notes at 132 or 138 on the metronome? To perform such a part, you will need to draw upon techniques and abilities beyond those of average players. While I was attending a music camp one summer, teachers began searching for me after noticing that I had been missing for several hours. I was eventually spotted, emerging from a small practice hut in the woods. It was 8:00 p.m. and I had gone the extra mile, putting in an eight-hour day of practice. I vividly remember learning a great deal that day, as I did on all the other days when I put in my typical five hours of practice time, and gained a great amount of satisfaction from the mastery of challenging passages ever since.

Tactic 3: Making It to the Practice Room

One other tactic I use is surprisingly simple. When I lack motivation, I visualize my body going one direction, while my head remains right where it is. For example, if I am surfing online, I physically move toward my practice area even if I am not mentally ready to do so. I enter the practice room, assemble my instrument, and begin to play, even while lacking the desire to practice at that moment. After a short while, I become engrossed in my music, and the creativity begins to flow.

Tactic 4: Three Steps Ahead

You can do a few things to expedite your practice routine.

Step 1: Reeds. Make sure you have reeds that are ready to play at a moment's notice. Playing clarinet is challenging, so it is important to avoid struggling with new reeds at the beginning of each session. Set aside some time every other day to prepare your reeds so you can practice without obstacles.

Step 2: Equipment. Naturally, you will be a step ahead if your equipment works well. Find the best setup possible (instrument, mouthpiece, reeds, and ligature), and have your instrument maintained by a repair technician on a regular basis.

Step 3: Practice Space. Keep your practice space clean and tidy so you can save time and find everything you need, such as your music, reeds, pencil, tuner, and metronome. If you prefer apps, avoid being distracted by your smartphone while using them.

Coda

As a professional clarinetist, I continue to practice every day to keep in shape. I do not put the clarinet away while on vacation. I chose to be a musician and believe that daily practice is part of my job. Dedication to one's career is essential, especially in professions that can be described as a "calling" such as in the arts, sciences, sports, and leadership positions. I live by this principle: "Work hard and things will come to you." The payoff is in the confidence that I can handle the difficult music that will inevitably come my way. The time to prepare is now. The fulfillment begins tomorrow.

SECRET 63: PLAYING POSTURE

Sitting

Good posture is very important in the sitting position and is critical for satisfactory body alignment and air control. A posture that shows alertness and professionalism sits well with conductors because it demonstrates your attention and readiness to perform under their direction.

Sit with a straight back and open up your torso/leg angle to 45 degrees instead of 90 degrees by lowering *one* of your legs. This will improve lung capacity and airflow by emulating the standing position. Play with your clarinet at a 35-degree angle and keep the head/neck at a 90-degree angle by looking straight ahead, as shown in fig. 63.1. Poor sitting position minimizes airflow because organs push against the diaphragm.

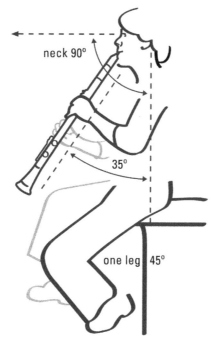

Figure 63.1

Standing

In a standing position, however, the lungs and diaphragm have more freedom to move properly. Standing up allows more airflow. Surprisingly, it takes a lot of abdominal and back muscle strength to sit up straight or stand up for an extended period of time. Activities such as yoga and pilates are excellent ways to improve core muscle strength and posture.

SECRET 64: RECORDING YOUR PRACTICE SESSIONS

Recording your practice sessions gives you the opportunity to act as your own teacher. Hiring yourself as your own teacher is not only a clever timesaver, it is a sure bet, and free of charge. Students often avoid recording their practice sessions because they dislike hearing themselves. However, what they hear is what the teacher or audience will hear later on. Wouldn't it make more sense to record passages repeatedly and make adjustments until you are happy with the result, ultimately increasing the likelihood that listeners will concur? When practicing, it is a challenge to objectively assess progress for several reasons:

1. The way you hear yourself internally is very different from how you really sound, so recording your practice sessions allows you to hear yourself as others hear you.
2. While practicing, you may overlook some details because you are busy concentrating on technical problems or playing the correct notes. Even when playing passages over and over, chances are that some details will be neglected, which can eventually affect the outcome of an audition or a performance. Naturally, it does take a little bravery to record your playing, and even more nerve to listen to the result. Moreover, it takes patience because recording yourself requires you to pause between passages in order to operate the device. If you are pressed for time, you might prefer to simply skip the recording process, but ultimately we play to be heard, so it is important to practice in a setting that emulates a live performance. The audio recorder is a great tool to reveal small details that can get past us while practicing, such as intonation subtleties or tempo variations.
3. Using a video recorder is also a great idea, however there are times when concentrating strictly on audio allows for fewer distractions when analyzing specific technical or musical issues.
4. Instrumentalists can be so busy playing that they are "hearing" but not really *listening*. Recording yourself makes you more aware of your playing, which makes you a much better listener and critical thinker. In time, you will be able to evaluate your playing more efficiently and accelerate your progress.

A full circle is established when we do the following:

- play
- assess our playing
- take corrective action
- repeat the passage with more awareness

High-quality portable digital audio recorders (as opposed to very inexpensive voice recorders) are readily available. Electronic devices can become obsolete in a matter of just a few months so it is important to do research, read reviews, and choose wisely before any purchase. Here are some tips for recording your practice sessions:

1. Listen and evaluate your playing by making note of your observations.
2. Hear notes before your fingers play them and pay attention to details in tone, articulation, rhythm, intonation, phrasing, and air speed variation. Always "dress up" your tone as if you were playing in a concert hall.
3. Use a metronome to assess your progress with technique and tonguing tempos. Keeping track of maximum tempos achieved while maintaining clean playing results in measurable progress.
4. Listen to professional recordings of music you are practicing and try to emulate the overall result.
5. Record yourself in various situations such as solo playing, duo with piano accompaniment, and with large ensembles. Remember to ask for permission before recording other musicians.
6. Record as you practice with play-along accompaniments or SmartMusic® online.
7. After listening to your recording a few times during your practice session, wait a few days to clear your mind and listen once again with a fresh set of ears.
8. File, organize, and back up your recordings in chronological order. You can then listen to your progress and assess variables such as speed, tone, and phrasing. Over time, your collection of sound files will be sizable and will clearly demonstrate your progress.
9. After a year or so, choose one audio file from your modest beginnings and a later file, recorded after months of hard work. Have your practice partners listen to and compare your "before and after" sound files. The progress demonstrated will undoubtedly convince interested parties to emulate your journey.

QUICK-TIPS BULLETIN BOARD—MUSICIANSHIP

- To keep tempo, tap your foot in your *soul*, not your *sole*.
- When you play *tutti* passages in orchestra, band, or large groups, every instrument should exaggerate short articulations to result in the entire group sounding precise and clean.
- Listen to high-level professional clarinet recordings or live concerts as much as possible to learn about and emulate phrasing, articulation, and tone.
- When the date of a solo performance approaches, practice while wearing your concert clothes to be prepared for this facet of the concert days in advance.
- Hear the pitch of notes in your mind before your fingers play them.
- Accelerando (as opposed to rushing) is good because it adheres to the mathematical equation of acceleration (perfectly gradual), therefore it sounds more natural than rushing (randomly gradual).
- Practice playing very lyrically and musically without moving your body to see if you can execute expressive phrases with your mind without the help of extra movements. Once you have achieved this, incorporate appropriate and natural body motion to enhance your performance.
- Avoid being a "practicer." Although it is imperative to repeat passages multiple times to improve muscle memory, a player who plays sections over and over can end up learning errors that are difficult to undo later. Instead, play a passage and analyze its content so it becomes logical and easier to execute in the long run. Practicing intellectually instead of physically will help you remember the difficult runs more clearly the next day. I call this "thinkology."
- If you can get to the point of actually forgetting the clarinet while you play and only hear the music, you are on your way to mature musicianship.

CHAPTER 6

Reeds and Equipment

SECRET 65: BREAKING IN A NEW CLARINET

It is important to carefully break in a new wood clarinet to diminish the risk of cracking (this also applies to an older instrument that has been stored for a long period of time). Wood is an organic material and will respond to various temperatures and humidity by swelling or shrinking. Breaking in your clarinet slowly will help the wood adapt to climate changes. To avoid excessive moisture absorption by the wood, refrain from playing a new instrument for prolonged sessions. This will reduce swelling and the potential for cracking.

It is also important to prevent the instrument from becoming too dry. In very dry climates, some players keep a few fresh orange peels inside the case (away from the keys) to maintain consistent, but low-level moisture. This is preferable to commercial products that can leak water in the case. Before breaking in your clarinet, I suggest coating the bore of your instrument with bore oil (see Secret 81: Bore Oil). Although opinions differ considerably, my preference is to seal the wood with the oil before playing (only use bore oil specifically designed for woodwind instruments). This will not necessarily prevent cracking, but it will limit quick swelling (excess moisture) or shrinkage (excess dryness). The steps to breaking in your clarinet are as follows:

1. Let your instrument adjust to the room's temperature before playing. If the room is cold, warm the top joint under your arm instead of blowing warm air through the bore.
2. During the first week, play the instrument fifteen minutes a day and silk-swab it thoroughly after each session.
3. During the second week, increase your playing time to two separate sessions of fifteen minutes a day. If you cannot play twice a day, increase the playing time by five minutes daily.

4. During the third week and beyond, increase the duration of your sessions each day.

Never leave your clarinet in a car during any season. Heat and cold could do serious damage, not to mention that leaving your instrument unattended increases the risk of theft. Avoid storing your instrument in cold lockers or near heat sources. If your instrument will be unused for some time, leave your case open to prevent mold growth.

Repairing a cracked clarinet can be costly, so it is best to take precautions. If cracking does occur, take your instrument to a trusted repair technician as soon as possible. Cracks can be pinned seamlessly and effectively.

SECRET 66: SELECTING A MOUTHPIECE

An inexpensive way to upgrade the performance of your clarinet is to invest in a professional-grade mouthpiece. Here are some selection pointers:

- Avoid buying a mouthpiece just because a renowned artist plays one. Everyone's embouchure, physical characteristics, and abilities are different, so the same mouthpiece will not necessarily yield the same results for everyone.
- A good mouthpiece will be easy to play, provide stability and consistency in pitch and tone in all registers, project well, have a "ring," articulate clearly, and generally not chirp or squeak.
- If you plan on taking lessons with a new teacher, make sure the teacher agrees with your setup to avoid another switch once your lessons begin.
- A long facing (surface against which the reed vibrates) requires less lung and diaphragm control and more lip control than a short facing. This setup typically works well with harder reeds and is often favored by orchestral players.
- A short facing requires less lip control and more breath control. This setup usually works well with softer reeds and is often chosen by jazz players.
- A medium facing usually works for most young players. It is easier to play in all registers and it works well with medium strength reeds. I usually recommend this option first, and then proceed with other options if needed.
- When trying a new mouthpiece, check intonation in all registers with a tuner.
- Beware of "love at first sight" when trying mouthpieces. Play pieces from your repertoire rather than simply playing your warm-up runs. Reality will set in when you play repertoire rather than random (and favorite) notes. Play each mouthpiece for a reasonable amount of time and in various settings (solo, ensemble) to see if the perceived air resistance increases significantly after several minutes of playing.
- Try as many mouthpiece brands as possible. Once you find a model that works well, try two or three samples of the same model since there may be slight variations in manufacturing.
- Enlist the help of your peers. Play each mouthpiece without revealing brand names, and see if the majority agrees with your choice.

A great way to increase shopping success is to find mouthpiece vendors who offer special trial plans. You can also attend a music or clarinet conference where a large number of vendors gather in one place for a few days. Once you have tried various facings for each brand, try them with different reed strengths. The idea is to find an ideal mouthpiece and reed combination. Choosing professional-quality reeds completes the equation.

SECRET 67: MOUTHPIECE PATCH

There are two schools of thought regarding whether or not to use a mouthpiece patch. One point of view recommends using one to reduce the amount of vibration against the upper teeth, to improve the grip on the mouthpiece with the teeth for increased embouchure stability, and to protect the mouthpiece surface from sharp teeth (see fig. 67.1). The flip side discourages use of a mouthpiece patch because it might inadvertently tame down the mouthpiece vibration, inhibiting response in general.

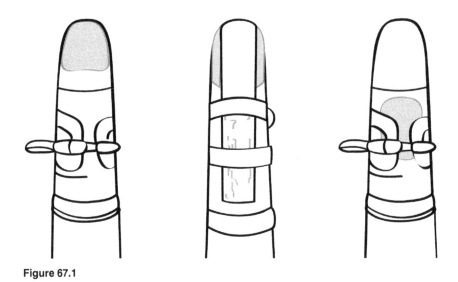

Figure 67.1

The decision depends upon physical characteristics and preferences. A patch will add about 0.5 mm in overall thickness to the mouthpiece, forcing the jaw into a slightly more open position. This could affect tongue control and increase tension, as the teeth are held farther apart. A good demonstration of this effect is to compare fast tonguing with a "dee" and "dah" syllable while speaking instead of tonguing on the tip of the mouthpiece. Invariably, the staccato speed will increase with the "dee" syllable because there is less jaw movement and tongue tension while the mouth is closed compared to when it is more open.

A compromise between the two practices would be to cut the mouthpiece patch in half and install the smaller patch to ensure grip but also allow more tonal response. Some people like to use black electrical tape instead of a specifically designed patch. I do not recommend this, as the taste is unpleasant and the tape might contain harmful ingredients that are unsafe for consumption. Additionally, the adhesive on this tape can soften after a few days and slip. Here are additional ways to use patches:

- No-bite trainer: Cutting small rectangular or half-moon shaped pieces and placing them on either side of the reed creates an elevated surface that is flush with the reed. Playing with these helps prevent biting because the new temporary "elevators" keep the teeth off the reed. This should be used only as a training device.
- Ligature anti-slip: Install a patch over the mouthpiece's logo to prevent the ligature from slipping upward.
- Upper-teeth position trainer: To avoid taking in too much upper mouthpiece, install a half patch slightly away from the mouthpiece tip to stop the upper teeth from sliding down. The upper teeth will rest on the unpatched mouthpiece tip (not shown in the figure).

Mouthpiece patches eventually wear out and can easily be replaced. When necessary, simply remove the old patch, clean the surface by rubbing the extra glue off with your thumb, and affix a new patch.

SECRET 68: TOOL-FREE REED PREP

Choosing and preparing commercial reeds can be a quick and simple process. Since reed-manufacturing machinery is calibrated to cut the cane to a specific size and shape that presumably produces near-perfect reeds, there is not much material left to remove, so in theory, no major work is needed. The goal is to prepare and have four concert-quality reeds on hand at all times with no reed adjustments or tools, and to enjoy playing right away.

The objective of this technique is not to economize and save ineffective reeds, but to choose from a pool of five to ten reeds so that you can select the best ones for immediate use. A reed that is good one day might not necessarily play well the next day, so the idea is to select a reed that will play well during the current practice session and also last for many practice sessions.

Materials Needed

1 clarinet
1 mouthpiece
1 ligature
10 brand new reeds
1 pencil

Day 1

1. Open a new box of ten reeds. Unpack five reeds, and leave the remaining reeds aside.
2. Put reed no. 1 in your mouth and wet it entirely on both sides and both ends with your tongue. Do not soak reeds in water, as they will saturate too quickly.
3. Hold the reed on the mouthpiece with your thumb and play an open g. To save time, do not use the ligature yet. Play a long note and several detached notes; you can tell if a reed is going to be good right away if your tonguing sounds great from the onset. Once you have determined that the reed responds well, tighten the reed with the ligature and play a short warm-up routine for about fifteen to twenty seconds.
4. If the reed is very good, check-mark your reed with a pencil.
5. Set it aside to dry on a table, face up.
6. Take reed no. 2, repeat steps 2–5.
7. If reed no. 2 is promising but not top notch, put the ligature on and play a short warm-up routine. Mark the "maybe" reed with a dot.

8. Take reed no. 3, repeat steps 2–5, and so on.

9. After testing five reeds, place each reed in order of preference, flat side up.

10. Play each check-marked reed once again for two minutes; if they are still playing well, place them face up to dry on a surface for two minutes, and rub dry each reed gently on the back of your arm before storing them. Do not store a water-saturated reed, as it will either ruin it or reduce its lifespan.

11. Play the remaining reeds from your five-reed batch that you marked with a dot for four minutes rather than only two minutes. Assess whether or not the dot-marked reeds are getting better.

12. When the five reeds have been tried, played, left to dry on a surface, and gently rubbed dry, you can store them in your favorite reed container. Do not put the reeds back in the original cardboard box, as they need to be in an environment that enables them to stay flat, and not warp. To extend the reeds' lives, choose a container that provides a humidity-stable environment, such as a Vandoren Hygro Case.

13. If you only found two or three very good reeds among the five reeds, unpack the remaining five reeds, and proceed with steps 2–5. Devote ten minutes for each batch of five reeds.

14. If a reed sounds unacceptable or fuzzy (there are always one or two in a box), put it aside, as it may play well a few months later.

Day 2

Play your check-marked reeds (your best reeds) for five to ten minutes. Do not overplay them, otherwise they will become saturated with moisture, start becoming too soft, and lose their playability. Also practice with the dotted reeds as long as desired.

Day 3

1. Play your check-marked reeds (your best reeds) for twenty minutes.

2. Rearrange your reeds in order of preference.

3. If the dotted reeds eventually become concert-level reeds, change your marking to a check-mark. The dotted, "promising" reeds might have more room to grow, and you can play them for a longer period of time. If a reed does not improve after three days, abandon it and start the process all over again with the remaining five new reeds.

4. Play your reeds in a rotation in order to lengthen their lifespans.

5. Also practice with the previously prepped reeds you stored a week prior, as long as desired.

The goal is to have three or four great-sounding reeds at all times. Any reed can change or deteriorate for no reason, but if you have several good reeds on hand, it is unlikely that *all* of them will change. This time-saving method requires no equipment and allows you to continuously replenish your supply of fresh, playable reeds.

SECRET 69: POSITIONING YOUR REED

As mentioned next in Secret 70: Express-Speed Reed Balancing, one way to ad-just reeds is by scraping the right and left sides with reed rush until both sides are balanced. Balancing reeds with reed rush is a quick, practical, and inexpensive method when pressed for time, such as in the middle of a rehearsal. I found that *before* scraping, one preliminary quick step can be taken that involves no tools whatsoever.

To find out whether your reed's sides respond evenly after properly positioning the reed on the mouthpiece, push it slightly to the side and test it. If the left side is too hard, slide the reed slightly to the right, as shown in fig. 69.1, and vice versa. After comparing both sides, determine if your reed response has improved enough so you will not need to make any permanent adjustments with reed rush or a knife.

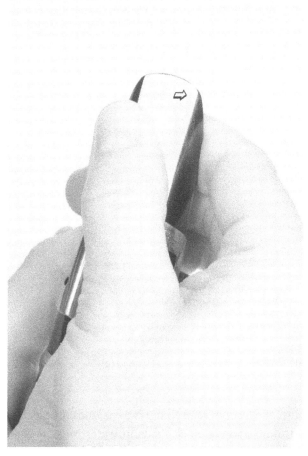

Figure 69.1

SECRET 70: EXPRESS-SPEED REED BALANCING

There are numerous methods to fix reeds. Some techniques require the use of several tools and demand a lot of time and practice. A number of clarinetists go a step further and make their own reeds from scratch. At the advanced stage of reed making, one typically will look at the cane's condition through a light source and even measure its thickness with a dial micrometer to ensure proper balance. I believe it is indeed necessary for clarinetists to know all the steps of reed making in detail as well as the many different adjustment techniques.

Once an advanced clarinetist has had some experience in reed making, it is also important to be able to quickly adjust reeds in time-critical situations. The express-speed reed-balancing technique is intended for such moments and is meant to enhance the entire spectrum of reed-fixing techniques. The only tool needed is reed rush.

Rather than *looking* at each side of the reed through a light source to see if it is balanced, this technique involves *listening* to the reed's sides (or "wings") instead. Figure 70.1 shows a reed that has been divided into three important parts: left side (indicated by L), right side (R), and heart (H).

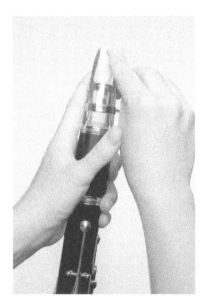

Figure 70.1

The most important aspect of reed fixing is to balance the sides so they will both respond evenly. Before playing, soak reeds in water for two or three minutes to help unwarp dry cane. To check the reed's balance, play an open g and, *without modifying your embouchure position whatsoever*, slightly rotate the instrument toward your left side (counterclockwise), therefore blocking the left side's reed vibration. You are now playing and listening to the right side of the reed *only*. Follow by turning the instrument to your right side (blocking the right side's reed vibration) and listen to the *left* side. Play each side separately, and compare both sides' sound and response. Any imbalance will become very clear once you evaluate both sides with your *ears* instead of your eyes. One side might feel much more resistant than the other. Once you determine which side needs adjustment, take a piece of reed rush and place it flat against the reed surface. Gently and evenly scrape the surface marked "L" or "R" until reed dust starts to appear. Play the reed once again and see if there are any changes in the response of the corrected side. Do not scrape too much cane off as this becomes irreparable. Instead, make slight changes and repeat the steps of playing and scraping several times until both sides are *almost* even. If you balance both sides 100 percent equally, the reed will become too soft almost right away. Time will correct slight imperfections, so it is best not to overdo it. Never touch the heart of the reed.

Repeat the above steps the next day. Additional adjustments may be needed on the third day. With a pencil, write a descriptive mark on the bottom part of the face of the reed (instead of the back) to avoid having to turn it over to read. Marking reeds helps to develop a sense of "statistics" to show how each reed reacts to various adjustments.

Balancing reeds this way saves time because there is no need to remove the reed from the mouthpiece during any stage of the technique. Moisture residue and skin particles form a hard crust and clog reed pores when drying, so it is a good idea to gently wash each reed with tap water after playing for an extended period of time.

SECRET 71: REED CLIPPER

A reed clipper is a handy tool to make the most out of soft reeds. It is used to trim the tip of a reed to remove imperfections and make the tip thicker. There are very few brand options, so it is a good idea to scan the market in case new models become available.

I recommend the classic sturdy model made by Cordier, designed for right-handed clipping (see fig. 71.1). The Rigotti trimmer is more affordable and works well for left-handed users, however, it is less sturdy. The reed clipper has a fastener that secures the reed onto the flat surface and a screw or knob that precisely positions the reed for trimming.

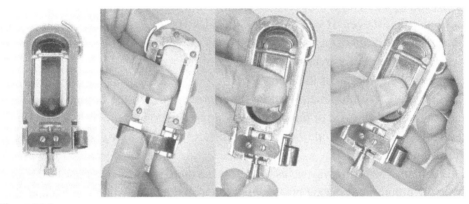

Figure 71.1

Once the reed is properly positioned, a small lever is pushed, which clips a sliver of cane off the tip. For best results, only a tiny amount of cane should be clipped. Following are the steps to clip a reed:

1. Unclip the lever and place the reed onto the flat part of the clipper. Close the fastener.
2. Turn the clipper around so you can see the reed tip and turn the screw either way until the reed slides just above the tip of the reed clipper's blade.
3. Push the lever until you hear a click and remove the reed from the clipper.

Using a clipper is likely to either save or ruin your reed. Therefore, be sure you are not too attached to the reed and willing to take the risk. It is best to practice using the clipper with a few old reeds before attempting to use it on a potentially good reed.

SECRET 72: REED RUSH

Reed rush (or Dutch rush or horsetail) is a small, thin, hollow plant with an abrasive surface that is used by clarinetists to scrape and adjust reeds. The plant usually grows along ponds or streams and is harvested, cut, and dried. Techniques on how to use reed rush are described in Secret 70: Express-Speed Reed Balancing.

Quality Control

A few companies harvest, prepare, and distribute reed rush. Look for reed rush that is cut evenly and boxed in a rigid and protective container (see fig. 72.1). The best pieces will be dark sage green, have a perfectly round and rigid cylindrical shape with clean edges, and be large enough in diameter to have contact with a significant amount of reed surface ("Good" in the figure).

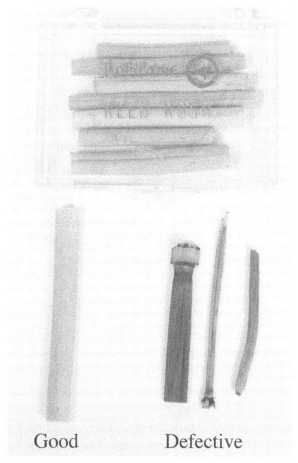

Good   Defective

Figure 72.1

Unfortunately, reed rush is sometimes sold in soft plastic bags and dried incorrectly, resulting in uneven pieces that are not trimmed or are too small to be effective. These pieces are often very dark and spotty, curved, too thin, and flat ("Defective" in the figure).

Choosing high-quality reed rush is financially judicious and will ensure a better outcome when working on your reeds.

Homemade Reed Rush

Since it grows along small bodies of waters, it is possible to acquire and process our own reed rush rather than to purchase the finished product. The first step to obtain reed rush is to find an area where the plant grows. I found mini-crops along rivers and creeks while taking walks in the woods in Ohio, as well as along trails in Indiana.

Harvesting and Cutting

The best time to harvest the stems is midsummer, when plants are large. Picking the plant when it is fully grown produces larger pieces that dry more evenly and are more desirable for reed work.

Harvest the plant by cutting the stems with sturdy scissors near the bottom of the plant, taking care not to harm the root, promoting future growth. Avoid picking pieces that have dark spots, as brown fluid might seep out and stain your fingers. Trim away the unusable thin top sections and buds.

Cut pieces three to four inches long. Cutting the reed rush *after* it is dried can result in cracked edges. The rings are not well suited for reed work, so make the cuts accordingly and discard the ring sections. On the other hand, if you want to use as much of the plant as possible and the dimensions allow it, you may leave one ring in the middle of each section rather than cutting it out (see fig. 72.2).

Drying

The most challenging part of preparing reed rush is getting the stems to remain round and stiff while drying. Reed rush appears to be dry when you pick it; however, freshly cut reed rush contains a surprising amount of moisture. It is best to bake the stems early on before they become wrinkled, soft, and flat.

Reed rush can be dried in either a microwave oven or a conventional oven. To use the microwave method, place about a dozen precut reed rush pieces on a paper towel and microwave them in increments of ten seconds. Replace the damp paper towel after each cycle and move the pieces around with a utensil to allow

 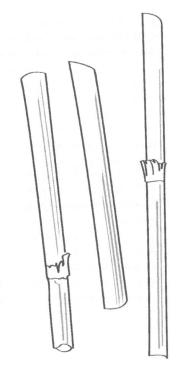

Figure 72.2

them to dry evenly. Let the pieces rest for a minute between each heating to allow evaporation.

The method works well, but it does require constant supervision. A word of caution: this method dries the plant very quickly so leaving it in the microwave too long could result in the reed rush catching on fire. Be careful when handling the heated pieces and use a utensil, as the natural oils and moisture in the plant can burn your fingers. Note that any pieces with rings should be baked in a conventional oven, as the sections between the rings will pop apart in a microwave oven. Place the reed rush on a paper towel instead of a plate because the plant's moisture collects on the plate's surface, making it necessary to wipe it dry it between each cycle.

My preferred method is using a conventional oven. Preheat the oven around 175 degrees or 200 degrees Fahrenheit (80–90 degrees Celsius), and then spread out two or three dozen precut reed rush pieces on a cookie sheet. Bake for about forty-five minutes, depending on the type of oven (electric, gas, convection) and stem sizes. Shake the cookie sheet every ten minutes or so and turn over the pieces with a spatula to accelerate evaporation. Make sure the stems are bone dry before turning off the oven, and use a timer for safety. Do not leave the pieces unattended or forget to remove them from the oven.

Let the pieces set for twenty minutes, then check for rigidity by gently rolling your fingers around each piece. Discard the ones that break or crack as well as the pieces that did not dry properly nor retain their round shape. Both microwave and conventional oven techniques tend to give off a pungent odor for a short time.

Storing

Once your chosen pieces of reed rush are dry and rigid, store them in small, protective containers. When dry, the pieces are ready to be used right away. Remember to share the wealth with your clarinet and saxophone friends and colleagues. They will appreciate the gesture.

SECRET 73: SYNTHETIC REEDS

As synthetic reed technology keeps improving, music educators are increasingly using them in their band programs, and more clarinetists choose to play them on a regular basis. Granted, the tone produced by a superior cane reed is hard to emulate. On the other hand, the time needed to find, break in, and fix cane reeds can turn a practice day into a reed-fixing day. Synthetic reed manufacturers do not recommend modification of the reeds, that is, no sanding, clipping, or scraping. Therefore, performers who would prefer to spend fewer hours fixing reeds might want to take a closer look at synthetic reeds.

Synthetic reeds are available from several manufacturers, including Avalar, Avante, Bari, Bravo, Fibracell, Forestone, Hartmann, Kleer Kane, Légère, and E.M. Reed. Légère reeds are immensely popular and have been adopted by top virtuoso professionals such as Ricardo Morales, principal solo clarinetist with the Philadelphia Orchestra. These reeds are made of oriented polypropylene and, just like cane, are stiffer in the longitudinal direction and have the same density as moistened cane.

As with cane reeds, one needs to take time to find the correct reed/mouthpiece combination for optimal results. Additionally, synthetic reeds do vary from one reed to another, so it is a good idea to acquire more than one or two. As with any product, preferences vary, so it is worth the investment to experiment with different strengths.

Once you decide what fits your needs, keep in mind that temperature can affect the reed's performance. Synthetic reeds get warmer as you play them, so they might become too soft at some point. I recommend having two reeds on hand and alternating them as needed. While the first reed cools down, it returns to its initial state and can be played just a few minutes later.

If you pause during practice or performance, it is best to either take the reed off the mouthpiece or loosen the ligature and lift the reed slightly off the mouthpiece to allow it to cool down. If the reed stays wet on the mouthpiece for an extended period, it might close up and not play at all until it dries. Incidentally, compared to cane reeds, Légère reeds are more resistant to the warping issue that is exacerbated by the larger surface area of bass clarinet reeds.

I find that using synthetic reeds is a huge time saver. The tone and feel might not be identical to cane, but with diligent experimentation, they can result in a beautiful tone and a less stressful reed experience.

Figure 73.1

SECRET 74: INSTALLING AN INSTANT NECK-STRAP RING

Clarinetists sometimes use a neck strap during practice or performance. More and more players consider this option after developing wrist pain due to excessive tension. Naturally, it is best to correct the problem at its root and consult a specialist if such a predicament occurs.

To prevent injury, warm up the body before each practice session. Gently rotate the wrists, arms, shoulders, and upper body to enhance blood circulation and to condition the muscles and joints to execute repetitive movements more safely.

If a neck strap is preferred, however, the instrument must be equipped with a ring on the thumb rest to hold the strap in place. If your instrument does not have a thumb rest ring, here is a very inexpensive and quick way to install your own. You will need:

1 "O" ring (rubber)
1 nylon spacer (rigid thick nylon)

Both items are available in various sizes. Bring your instrument to the hardware store and experiment with various combinations until you find what works for your thumb rest. Then, place the rubber ring around the clarinet's thumb rest (see fig. 74.1).

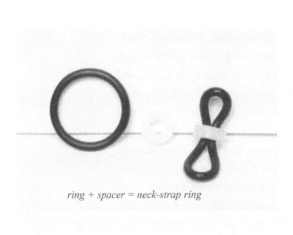

ring + spacer = neck-strap ring

Figure 74.1

Push down the nylon spacer to secure the ring tightly around the thumb rest. Insert the neck-strap hook in the upper part of the rubber ring, and voilà! You are done.

The second figure shows the thumb rest wrapped with a thumb cushion. I recommend choosing a rather soft, "gummy" thumb rest for optimal comfort. Also, the gummy quality helps to prevent the instrument from slipping or shifting from the thumb while playing.

Lastly, it is important to choose a neck strap specifically made for the clarinet, as saxophone neck straps tend to be too long for clarinet playing.

SECRET 75: MOLESKIN PADDING

It is surprising how many unlikely materials and products clarinetists can use for instrument repairs and improvements. One of these products is Dr. Scholl's Molefoam Padding, a dense felt material backed with a strong adhesive (figure 75.1, A). Generic brands (B) are thinner. Here are three ways to use the material:

1. Keep reeds moist inside the mouthpiece cap and reed case (C).
2. Lower the pitch of clarion B (D).
3. Substitute for key cork.

Figure 75.1

Keeping the reed moist when practicing, playing, or teaching over the course of several hours is a great way to ensure that your reed's response stays consistent throughout the day. As shown in the figure, trim a rectangular piece and place it in the mouthpiece cap facing the reed to keep it damp. The adhesive is very effective, but it can also be easily removed when it is time to replace it with a fresh new piece, which lasts about a month. To moisten the pad, pat some water on the pad with your fingers. To avoid rust, use a plastic cap (fig. 75.1, C).

When your clarion b^1 (third line on staff) is consistently sharp, place a rectangle of padding in the bell. Be careful that the piece is not so large that the low E becomes flat (D). Lastly, use very small squares as quick replacements for key corks. Additional uses are limited only by your imagination.

SECRET 76: TAPE IN TONE HOLE

Clarinetists face interesting intonation challenges due to the register hole serving double function with the B♭ throat note. The register tone hole is too large for register notes (therefore they tend to be sharp); however, it is too small to allow the throat B♭ to sound resonant. Closing extra holes when playing throat notes helps darken the tone and lowers the pitch, and refraining from biting helps flatten the register notes' intonation. In some cases, however, a small procedure can help lower the pitch on notes that are usually quite sharp, such as the clarion e¹ (fourth space on the staff). Since a smaller tone hole results in a lower pitch, tape can be added in the tone hole to fix the problem.

Before starting, make sure to clean the surface inside the tone hole with a damp cotton swab to ensure adherence of the tape. The following steps are illustrated in figure 76.1.

1. Cut a 1.25-inch (3.2 cm) piece of white first-aid tape (A). This kind of tape is waterproof and is thick enough to require only one layer. The tape can be trimmed to size once it is applied inside the tone hole. With experience, you will be able to closely estimate the length of tape required to encircle the diameter of the tone hole without overlapping. If intonation only needs minute correction, use a thinner kind of first-aid tape as shown in Secret 77: Tape Types.
2. Cut a thin piece that will fit into the tone hole, and trim the jagged edges if applicable (B).
3. With tweezers, apply the trimmed piece of tape into the tone hole evenly (C).
4. Make sure the tape covers the entire surface, however, avoid overlapping. This takes a little practice and can be mastered in a few attempts (D).
5. If you prefer the tape to remain invisible, apply black electrical tape. Since the black tape is thinner, two plies may be needed.
6. If a note is sharp, put the tape in the tone hole immediately below the last finger playing the note. For example, to flatten clarion e¹, apply the tape in the d¹ hole (right ring finger). To flatten clarion d¹, apply the tape in the F/c¹ right-hand little-finger tone hole (this requires removal of the key).

Naturally, it is much easier to add tape inside a hole not covered by a pad, however, with a little practice this can be achieved on most notes. Do not apply tape in very small holes, and only apply tape when a note is extremely sharp even when proper embouchure is used. Once applied to a clean surface, the tape should stay in place for years.

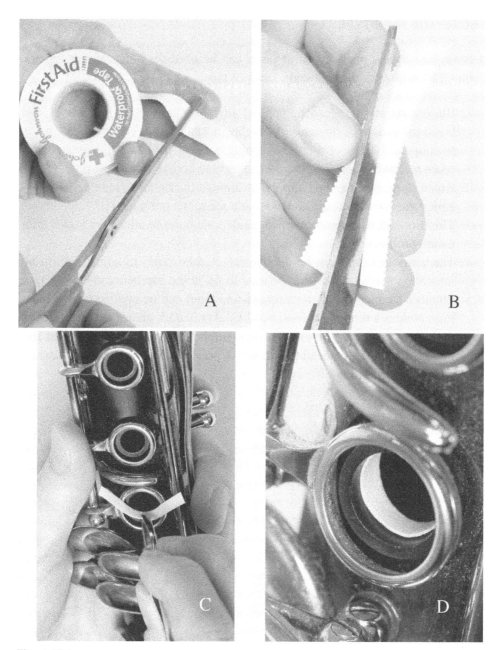

Figure 76.1

SECRET 77: TAPE TYPES

It is surprising how many types of tapes can be used for quick, minor repairs. Figure 77.1 illustrates the following kinds of tape:

1. Black electrical tape can be applied anywhere on the clarinet's body and blend in because of its color. A few layers can be applied underneath a key to temporarily replace a noise-reducing cork, or fill in a gap between keys when a cork falls off, or placed inside a tone hole to flatten the pitch (A).
2. Green floral tape can be temporarily applied over a loose joint cork. Apply cork grease over the tape and assemble the joints normally (B).
3. Thin first-aid tape can be applied inside tone holes to adjust for minor intonation problems (C).
4. Thick first-aid tape can be applied inside tone holes to adjust significant intonation problems or it can be used to fill in the gap between keys (E).
5. Plumber's tape (or Teflon or thread-seal tape) can be applied over a loose joint cork as a temporary fix (D and F). Apply cork grease on both sides of the tape to help it stay in place, and assemble the joints normally. It can also be rolled up over the metal thumb rest to prevent the thumb cushion inserted over it from slipping off.

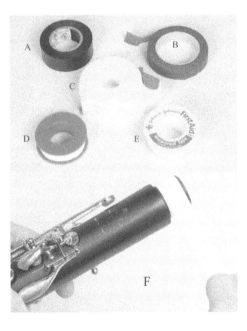

Figure 77.1

Some of the various kinds of tapes available can be a clarinetist's best friend in both routine and emergency situations. Exploring the possibilities for each one can save the day as well as improve your performance outcomes.

SECRET 78: VALENTINO SYNTHETIC CORKS

I believe in being an innovator.

—Walt Disney, American pioneer of animated films

In the past, it took a professional repairperson several hours to replace a clarinet joint cork. Thankfully, anyone can now do this repair in a few minutes using a synthetic, precut cork material made by Valentino and distributed by J. L. Smith & Co. The corks are easy to install and are more flexible than natural cork. Therefore, they fit better and last longer.

To replace a joint cork, remove the old cork and gently and carefully clean the area with a small screwdriver, blade, or similar tool. Remove the adhesive protective paper from the back of the synthetic precut cork, and tightly wrap the cork around the joint. Trim off the excess cork and save it for key work. The adhesive behind the cork is extremely effective and the cork will stay in place for years. Valentino cork products are shown in fig. 78.1: key corks in precut shapes (A) and joint corks (B). The joint corks can also be used for mouthpieces, and trimmings can be used for various key cork work.

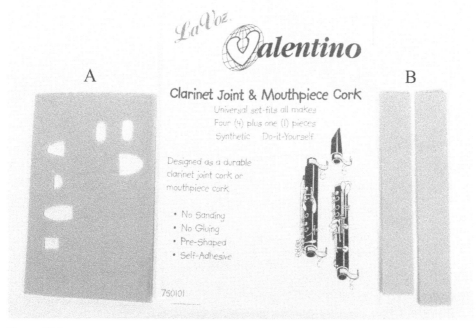

Figure 78.1

SECRET 79: SWAB REMOVAL TOOL

Because there is a metal register tube (or chimney) protruding inside the top part of the upper joint, it is important to be careful when pulling a swab through the bore of a clarinet. Insert the weighted pull slowly and make sure the swab is completely untangled before sliding it through the bore, verifying that the swab is not ripped or otherwise damaged beforehand. Silk swabs are thinner and slide more easily than cotton, so they are highly recommended. If for some reason your swab does get stuck in the bore, I suggest freeing it using a homemade tool with a harpoon-shaped tip.

How to Make a Swab Removal Tool

Purchase a thin, ten-inch-long (25 cm) flathead screwdriver and ask a key maker at the hardware store to grind the tip in the shape of a mini-harpoon, as shown in fig. 79.1. For best results, use a pencil on the screwdriver blade to outline the hook shape to be created.

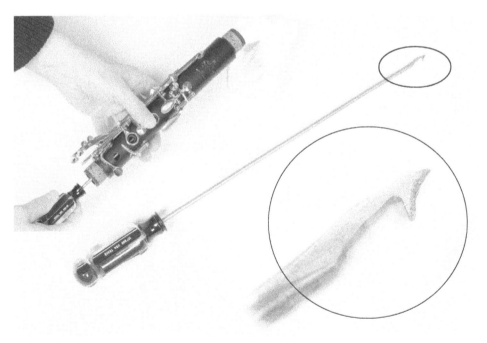

Figure 79.1

Removing the Swab

Insert the tool through the bottom of the upper joint, and twist the harpoon tip into the swab until it is hooked securely. Gently pull out the swab through the bottom part of the joint. Never try to pull the swab back through the top part of the joint and be careful not to scratch the wood (bore) during the process.

SECRET 80: EMERGENCY EQUIPMENT

Sooner or later, it happens to all of us. You arrive at a performance well prepared and on time. You take your seat on the stage to warm up, open your case, and discover that an important piece of equipment such as your mouthpiece or barrel is missing. We have all left our music or important equipment at home or in the practice room, resulting in panic and risk to our reputations as dependable musicians. I recommend that clarinetists keep numerous items in an emergency kit in their car, locker, or bag to help deal with unforeseen situations. Examples are listed below and can vary depending on individual needs.

- Spare mouthpiece and barrel: Since extreme temperatures will cause damage, you should not leave your best mouthpiece and barrel in your car. However, keeping inexpensive replacements in your car can be a lifesaver.
- Extra reeds: As with mouthpieces and barrels, extreme temperatures could damage reeds. As an extra precaution, synthetic reeds such as the excellent reeds made by Guy Légère can be added to the mix. These reeds are also particularly effective with auxiliary instruments like Eb piccolo clarinet and bass clarinet.
- Spare ligature: If you do not have a ligature or if your spare ligature breaks, adhesive tapes of any kind can be put around the mouthpiece and reed at the last minute.
- Small screwdriver set: Screws and keys can fall off or require adjustment due to weather changes.
- Self-adhesive pads: These are much quicker to install than regular skin pads.
- Rubber bands of various sizes: These can be used to temporarily repair weak or broken springs.
- A music stand light (with extra batteries): This is very useful when the performance space is not well lit or if you play a late afternoon outdoor event that continues as natural light fades. Always remember to angle the light away from the audience's eye level.
- Folding music stand: This is also useful to help out colleagues who are missing a music stand at the last minute.
- Clothespins: Snack bag clips or clothespins hold music in place at windy outdoor concerts.
- Sunglasses for outdoor concerts: If you play a late afternoon concert facing west on a sunny day, the sun will set right in your eyes.
- Earplugs: Brass instruments can sometimes sit close behind the clarinet section, potentially damaging your hearing in loud passages.
- Sewing kit: Concert attire may need last-minute sewing.
- Money: Always have extra cash hidden away in case of emergency.

Other extras include replacements for thumb rest cushions, reed rush, reed clipper, mini water container for reeds, folding scissors, adhesive tapes of all kinds, pencil, pad-drying paper, cork grease, and personal care items.

SECRET 81: BORE OIL

To Oil, or Not to Oil?

There are various opinions regarding whether or not one should oil the clarinet bore. Some repair technicians also recommend oiling the inside of tone holes. I believe that it is a good idea to simply oil the inside of the bore as a measure to prevent cracking, especially when the instrument is new.

The two main effects of oiling the bore may seem contradictory. Oiling the bore prevents the wood from drying out. On the other hand, it creates a barrier that prevents extra moisture such as water and saliva from penetrating the wood. The primary benefit of oiling the bore is that it helps stabilize the moisture content of the wood, which can prevent cracking. Additionally, it helps prevent water buildup in tone holes by facilitating the movement of water down the bore. Lastly, it can prevent the instrument's joints from shrinking and becoming loose. I suggest oiling the bore of a new clarinet a total of three or four times in the first year as follows:

1. Immediately upon purchasing a new instrument
2. Once after one week
3. Once or twice after three and five weeks

I believe it is not necessary to oil the bore after the first year. Note that some manufacturers advise against oiling the bore and doing so may void the warranty. Choosing whether to oil the clarinet bore is a personal decision. If done correctly, it can be an effective way to prevent the wood from cracking. Needless to say, never oil the mouthpiece and avoid playing on a freshly oiled instrument.

Applying Bore Oil

To begin, you need bore oil, a brush, some aluminum foil cut in squares (see fig. 81.1, A–D), and paper towels. You can use a brush made specifically for oiling the bore or a "pad saver" (A). If you wish to oil the inside of the tone holes, you will also need cotton swabs (this extra step requires removal of the keys). Use only bore oil that is specifically designed for woodwind instruments. Bore oil should never be used to oil the keys (use key oil instead).

Apply a very small quantity of oil by dribbling a thin dotted line onto the brush, spreading it evenly. One way to estimate the correct amount of oil is by testing the oiled brush on the barrel or bell, as there are no keys, pads, or holes. Insert the brush into the barrel and rotate it slowly back and forth. If oil drops appear, dab off excess oil with a paper towel.

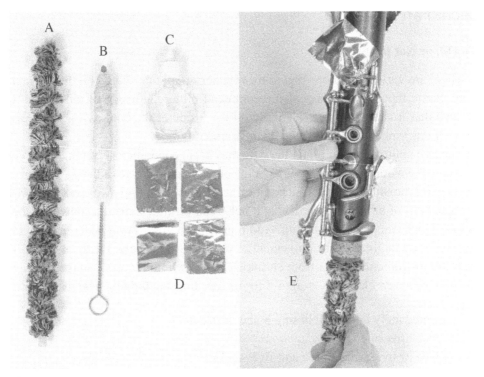

Figure 81.1

Before you oil the upper and lower joints, protect the pads by applying small aluminum foil squares over each hole that is covered by a closed pad (E). Oil the lower joint by carefully inserting the brush from the bottom, and avoid applying too much pressure so the oil won't drip from the brush. Be sure to evenly cover the entire bore surface.

Since the upper joint is partially blocked by a register hole chimney about 2 inches (5 cm) from the top, it is oiled in two steps—from the bottom and then from the top. After oiling the entire bore, leave the clarinet case open overnight for aeration. The next day, clean your instrument with a silk swab and check for any excess oil where the joints fit together and on pads and keys. Lastly, remove the aluminum squares. The instrument is now ready to be played.

SECRET 82: EZO TEETH CUSHION

Irritation inside the lower lip can occur after playing for an extended period of time. Once you have developed a consistent embouchure with minimal biting on the reed, a protective, flexible cushion can be placed over the lower teeth to minimize discomfort. This helps improve embouchure endurance by providing protection for the lower lip and it makes playing much easier in the high register. However, if this aid is utilized prematurely, it can encourage biting, which is undesirable for a good embouchure and full tone.

An effective solution is to use EZO denture cushions. Cut the cushions to size and fit over the lower teeth to help make extended practice sessions more comfortable. Figure 82.1 illustrates the various cutting steps from the original shape (A). First, cut a one-inch (2.5 cm) piece (B). Trim the edges for comfort (C). Fold the piece in half and place the cushion over the lower teeth and press into place with the tongue and fingers. EZO is made with wax and therefore body heat facilitates molding after a minute or two in the mouth (D). The material may be placed over braces and orthodontic appliances and can help with uneven teeth and smooth out sharp teeth that cut the inside of the lower lip. Once the material softens in the mouth, it is hardly noticeable while playing.

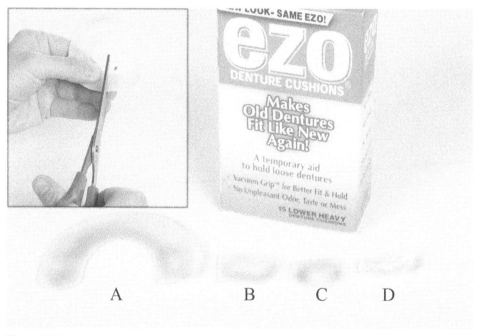

A   B   C   D

Figure 82.1

Because the material quickly dries once out of the mouth, carefully remove it from your teeth so that the shape remains intact and, for protection, store the dry piece in a small box with air holes for ventilation. If stored properly, a single piece can last for at least two weeks.

A word of caution: be careful when inhaling while using the cushion as it may dislodge and become a choking hazard. If molded properly on the teeth, it should remain in place, but safety should be the highest priority at all times.

QUICK-TIPS BULLETIN BOARD—REEDS AND EQUIPMENT

- I recommend installing a protective rubber cushion on the metal thumb rest for comfort. To prevent it from slipping off, apply plumber's Teflon tape (white thread-seal tape) around the metal thumb rest and place the thumb cushion over it.
- To prevent the thumb rest screws from loosening from the wood, apply a small amount of putty on the screw threads.
- Although it is tempting to fault the reed for a less-than-satisfactory sound, it is important to keep in mind that a clarinetist's job includes preparing and fixing reeds. Reed-fixing skills ultimately enhance your performance success.
- To keep track of your favorite reeds, place small stickers in shapes such as hearts or stars on the plastic reed holder or inside a reed case. Choose different color stickers to identify special characteristics such as concert-ready reeds, practice reeds, or jazz reeds.
- When assembling your instrument, make sure to verify that your forked, one-one fingering (left and right index fingers) seals tightly and that the pad below the left index finger is not leaking. If this fingering does not seal properly, some notes, including the forked E♭/B♭, will either squeak or not respond adequately.
- If a neck strap is used, verify that it is the correct length depending on your height and the neck strap ring's position on the instrument.
- Apply cork grease regularly to avoid wearing down mouthpiece and joint corks.
- When putting together your mouthpiece and joints, blow warm air on the greased corks to facilitate assembly.
- To pull apart stuck joints, slightly "click" them from side to side before twisting them apart.
- When cork grease fails and joints keep getting stuck or will not insert completely, gently sand the inside of the receiving joint with your index finger. Use very fine grit sandpaper and make sure the inside joint is free of cork grease beforehand. Avoid excessive sanding by continually checking tightness.
- Use a silk swab to clean your mouthpiece and instrument. Run the swab through the mouthpiece or joints slowly to avoid eroding the mouthpiece's baffle and the joints' inner walls, which can cause sharpness. Avoid cotton or

chamois swabs, as they are thicker and more abrasive. To dry the mouthpiece, insert the silk swab from the bottom up to protect the tip and edge rails.

- When trying new reeds, test them by playing a piece of music instead of your usual warm-up pattern. Players tend to subconsciously choose comfortable notes and articulations when warming up; however, the true reed response test comes when patterns are chosen by a composer instead.

- When choosing and breaking in new reeds, remember to play soft dynamics. Most reeds respond adequately when played loudly.

- To flatten a warped reed tip quickly, place the wet reed on the mouthpiece's table, and roll the hard side of your thumb back and forth over the tip of the reed.

- Use powder paper to eliminate sticky pads. Insert the paper gently between the tone hole and pad, close the pad, and press lightly on the pad while slipping the paper off. Repeat if necessary. Make sure to choose a powder paper specifically designed for woodwind pads, as other kinds (such as makeup powder paper) contain excessive amounts of talc and eventually exacerbate the problem. If proper powder paper is not available, thin, glueless, cigarette paper can be used instead.

- Insert a "reward if found" note along with your contact information or a GPS tracker in your clarinet case in the event you lose your instrument.

CHAPTER 7

Enhancing Repertoire

SECRET 83: BE THE FIRST TO PRACTICE
SECOND CLARINET ORCHESTRAL PARTS

Clarinetists who aspire to join a symphony orchestra spend years studying and practicing first clarinet parts from the orchestral literature. This is excellent preparation for a principal clarinet position, but what if the job opening is for second clarinet?

If clarinetists focus only on first clarinet parts during their studies, they will inevitably be at a disadvantage when a second clarinet position becomes available. It is illogical to prepare for a principal clarinet position in college, yet wait until the last minute to practice for a second clarinet position as a professional. Although most of us aspire to play first chair, many of the opportunities are for second part. Additionally, younger players would gain valuable experience playing second part for several years before moving into a principal position. Second clarinet audition repertoire lists do include some first clarinet parts (and most often the Mozart clarinet concerto), yet being proactive and mastering second clarinet parts early on is a great way to improve chances of being competitive for more auditions.

Although a few second clarinet parts are included in orchestral excerpt books, they are generally hard to find. Check various professional orchestral websites to see if they post audition repertoire parts for the positions of Associate Principal, Assistant Principal, or Second Clarinet. Note that these positions usually include E♭ piccolo clarinet duties (see Secret 84: E♭ Piccolo Clarinet). Other sources of second clarinet parts are university, community, and professional orchestral libraries, as well as *The Orchestra Musician's CD-ROM Library*, which includes a large selection of complete first and second clarinet parts.

Playing second clarinet in an orchestra is not for everyone. It requires special skills like respectful cooperation, willingness to take criticism, flexibility, and ability to match the principal clarinet in style, tone, and intonation. Second clarinet parts typically include more rests than first parts so it is important to develop a long attention span for counting rests.

Lastly, playing second clarinet requires humility to accept that most often the credit and accolades will be directed toward the principal player. The upside is that there is a lot to be said for being part of it all with virtually none of the solo stress. Also, in contrast with other woodwinds such as the flute, oboe, and bassoon, the clarinet is the most suited to play "second" because of how easily the low register responds on the instrument. For these reasons I see the second clarinet chair as one of the best seats on stage. The second clarinet excerpts most often found on audition lists include the following:

- Bartók's Concerto for Orchestra, Miraculous Mandarin Suite, and Symphonies Nos. 8 and 9
- Beethoven's Symphonies Nos. 2 (2nd movement), 5, 6, 8, and 9 (3rd movement)
- Berlioz's *Symphonie fantastique* (3, 4, 5)
- Brahms's Piano Concerto No. 2 (3), and Symphonies Nos. 2 (4), 3 (2), 4
- Britten's *Young Person's Guide to the Orchestra*
- Bruckner's Symphony No. 7
- Debussy's *La mer*
- Mahler's Symphony No. 4
- Mendelssohn's *A Midsummer Night's Dream, Fingal's Cave Overture (Hebrides)*, and Symphonies Nos. 3 and 4 (2, 4)
- Mozart's Symphony No. 39 (1, 2, 3)
- Rachmaninoff's Symphony No. 2 (3)
- Ravel's *Daphnis et Chloé* (Suites Nos. 1 and 2), and *Capriccio espagnol* (cadenza)
- Rimsky-Korsakov's *Scheherazade* and *Rapsodie Espagnole*
- Shostakovich's Symphonies Nos. 1 and 5 (3)
- Smetana's *Moldau*
- Strauss's *Till Eulenspiegel* and *Don Juan*
- Stravinsky's *Firebird* (1919) and *Petrouchka* (1947)
- Tchaikovsky's Symphony No. 5 (1st movement, opening)

SECRET 84: E♭ PICCOLO CLARINET

One way for a clarinetist to maximize performance opportunities is to become proficient on the E♭ piccolo (or sopranino) clarinet. Great parts have been written for the instrument in the wind symphony and military band repertoire. Important E♭ clarinet solos are found in orchestral repertoire, and while a significant portion of orchestral music written before the early 1900s included D clarinet parts, most have been transposed for E♭ clarinet.

Orchestral E♭ Clarinet Auditions

The process of preparing for an orchestral audition is complex, and essential steps include acquiring the appropriate sheet music and recordings, studying with a qualified teacher, planning a rigorous practice schedule, playing audition material for teachers and colleagues, and researching details about the audition process, audition space, and committee procedures. About a dozen excerpts are considered to be standard for E♭ clarinet. The most frequently requested are *Symphonie fantastique* (5th movement) by Berlioz; *Boléro*, *Daphnis et Chloé* (Suite No. 2), and Piano Concerto in G Major by Ravel; Symphonies Nos. 5 and 6 by Shostakovich; *Till Eulenspiegel* by Strauss; and *The Rite of Spring* by Stravinsky. Other excerpts include *El Salón México* by Copland; Symphonies Nos. 1, 6, and 9 by Mahler; Symphony No. 7 by Shostakovich; and *Also Sprach Zarathustra* and *Heldenleben* by Strauss. Some works require doubling on B♭, A, C, and even D clarinets, so it is important to have access to these instruments or to be prepared to transpose some sections. Aspiring professionals will usually purchase a set of B♭ and A clarinets early on; however, they may wait many years before investing in additional instruments.

Jonathan Gunn, professor of clarinet at the University of Texas at Austin and former associate principal and E♭ clarinetist with the Cincinnati Symphony Orchestra, offers the following advice:

1. Acquire the best instrument you can find. Also find a setup that is comfortable to play and not too stuffy. Often, E♭ novices get old instruments that are in poor shape and very difficult to play.
2. Experiment with many different equipment combinations (mouthpiece, barrel, ligature, reeds). If you cannot get E♭ reeds to work well, you may get better results by cutting off the butt end of a B♭ reed.
3. Learn every possible alternate fingering, especially in the high register. If you have trouble finding an in-tune fingering for a particular passage, try to create your own.

4. Train your ear and remain very flexible with pitch. It is crucial to be able to quickly adjust intonation.

5. Be able to vary the sound of the instrument. The E♭ clarinet does not always have to sound bright and shrill. Experiment with your tongue position. You may find that a tongue position that is ineffective for B♭ clarinet works very well on E♭.

6. Think small with your fingers. Use smaller movements and be extra careful to have a natural, curved finger position. When the fingers are flat it is especially difficult to cover the relatively small tone holes correctly.

7. Plan practice time carefully and avoid over-practicing immediately before an audition. Intense, last-minute E♭ practicing can result in excessive biting and a sore bottom lip.

8. Air support is crucial, so do not back off when you are unsure.

9. Be careful not to hunch over just because the instrument is small.

10. Above all be confident. Lack of confidence and the E♭ clarinet do not mix well.

SECRET 85: BASS CLARINET

Bass Clarinet Orchestral Audition Preparation

Another way for a clarinetist to maximize performance opportunities is to become proficient on bass clarinet. Increasing your versatility will make you a more marketable musician. Serious clarinet students would benefit from taking lessons from a professional bass clarinetist. Ed Palanker, former bass clarinetist with the Baltimore Symphony Orchestra, offers the following advice (see from here to the end of the Secret):

Few clarinetists own a bass clarinet, however, for orchestral auditions, it is necessary to own one that plays down to low C because many works from the standard orchestral repertoire require the added range. Since new bass clarinets are expensive, one should consider purchasing a used instrument. Bass clarinets present some maintenance problems including bending of the long rods, bridge keys, and the double-octave mechanism. Be sure to take special care when assembling and taking the instrument apart and keep the joints well greased.

Depending on personal interest, aspiring professional clarinetists may want to also acquire a number of auxiliary low clarinets such as a basset clarinet, basset horn, and contrabass clarinet. You can start practicing some easy B♭ clarinet etudes and work up to the Rose studies and more advanced books later on. Since many orchestral excerpts are written in bass clef, I suggest studying the original cello *Suites* by J. S. Bach as well as intermediate bassoon or cello etudes to become fluent in bass clef. Additionally, there is a considerable amount of music written for the bass clarinet in A, so it is a good idea to learn to transpose down a half-step.

Bass clarinetists are sometimes expected to play the assistant-first or second clarinet parts. So, if you are considering taking bass clarinet auditions, you must also be an accomplished soprano clarinetist.

Technique

Depending on the angle of the neck, you might have to hold the instrument at a slight angle. If you don't use a neck strap, hold the bell between your feet for support. Find a comfortable height, but do not bend your head down to reach the mouthpiece.

Fingerings are the same as on the soprano clarinet except for the lowest notes (different on various models), and the upper register has two sets of fingerings. Use the left-index-half-hole and alternate fingerings for the high register. High $c\sharp^2$ and d^2 can be played with or without the half-hole, whereas it is necessary above the high d^2. Fingering charts are available online and in bass clarinet method books such as *The Bass Clarinet* by Jean-Marc Volta, published by International Music Diffusion.

Orchestral Excerpts

There are about a dozen excerpts that are considered to be standard for auditions and they can be found in bass clarinet excerpt books. Some of the most common excerpts are *On the Trail* from the *Grand Canyon* Suite by Ferde Grofé, *Don Quixote* by Strauss, *La Valse* by Ravel, and *Piano Concerto* by Khachaturian.

Clarinetists will discover a whole new world of performance opportunities and musical experiences by adding bass clarinet to their skills. An experienced bass clarinet teacher can help you select repertoire, equipment, mouthpiece, and reeds, and give you the edge you need to succeed in your new endeavor.

SECRET 86: WOODWIND DOUBLING

A great way to multiply professional performance opportunities is by becoming a woodwind doubler. Clarinetists interested in increasing their marketability and playing myriad musical styles may want to study other woodwind instruments such as saxophone, flute, and oboe. Naturally, this requires a great deal of dedication on each instrument as well as a significant monetary investment. Also, it requires the study of techniques that might not be used on clarinet such as diaphragm vibrato, double reed making, or learning different styles of music such as baroque and jazz.

Clarinetist/saxophonist Dr. John Cipolla, professor of music at Western Kentucky University and Broadway musician in New York City for more than thirty years, offers the following advice (see from here to end of the Secret):

At the core of a doubler is someone who sincerely likes playing each instrument, as well as various styles of music, and one who can accept being a section player rather than a soloist. The best doublers are very detail-oriented people. Simply knowing how to play each instrument is not sufficient to succeed as a doubler. One must devote years of intense preparation and acquire the best possible equipment.

Equipment

Doublers need top-of-the-line instruments. Eventually, this may also mean purchasing auxiliary instruments such as piccolo, E♭ and bass clarinets, and various saxophones. This translates into a sizable financial commitment, but it can make the difference between your name landing on top of the call list or not.

Have a variety of mouthpieces that will suit different types of music, especially saxophone mouthpieces for jazz and classical. Precise intonation and clarity of response are difficult to maintain as a doubler because of the embouchure changes between instruments. Good equipment will help you get the most out of your abilities.

Reeds tend to dry out when an instrument rests on the stand, therefore, it is important to soak the large reeds (saxophones, bass clarinet) for at least ten minutes before the performance. Arrive at least an hour early to set up instruments and to allow for any delays. Warm up before arriving at the performance, and keep any reed adjusting and warming up very quiet once on site. Oftentimes, musicians are not rehired because they warm up with a full-volume concerto, disregarding the stage crew and other musicians who have plenty to do before the performance.

Most popular music ensembles are quite loud, and there is a risk of experiencing some hearing loss, therefore, it is imperative to learn to play with hearing protection. Buy foam or custom-molded musicians' earplugs that enable you to hear while you are playing. The next important step is to use earplugs while practicing so that you can get used to the difference in perceived sound.

Pre-professional Training

I recommend that students begin by mastering one instrument before moving on to others. When the time comes to learn other instruments, study each instrument with a professional teacher and practice each one for a minimum of one year (several hours of practice per day). This intensive preparation will enable you to sound as if each instrument is your primary instrument.

Performing Opportunities

Seek out small and large ensemble performance experiences. Ensembles offer doublers opportunities to hone their skills in the areas of style, rhythm, tuning, and blending. A great way to meet potential teachers is to join the musicians' union and contact some established members to ask if you can take lessons. This will give them an opportunity to hear you and ultimately recommend you for gigs.

Each performance is an unspoken audition for the conductor and other players who might recommend you for other jobs. Play recitals and chamber music on each instrument at local libraries, churches, and schools to gather experience.

Practicing

It can be a challenge to find enough hours during the day to practice multiple instruments, so manage your practice sessions wisely. Practice in short segments and plan what you will accomplish in each one.

Gain experience playing saxophone in a jazz band and listen to recordings and live performers to develop a genuine concept of sound. Additionally, study the baroque style on flute and oboe.

SECRET 87: MILITARY BAND AUDITIONS

Many career opportunities for instrumentalists are found in military bands. The advantages of these positions include diverse performance venues and repertoire, tuition support, loan repayment programs, medical benefits, extensive travel, attractive compensation, and government benefits.

Dr. Douglas Monroe, clarinet professor at East Carolina University, former commander and conductor in the U.S. Air Force Band, and former clarinetist with the U.S. Army Field Band in Washington, D.C., offers the following advice (see from here to the end of the Secret):

Each branch of the military has at least one premier band. Five of the eight bands are stationed in Washington, D.C.: the United States Army Band, the United States Army Field Band, the United States Navy Band, the United States Marine Band, and the United States Air Force Band. Other premier bands are the United States Naval Academy Band in Annapolis, Maryland; the United States Military Academy Band in West Point, New York; and the United States Coast Guard Band in New London, Connecticut.

In addition to the premier bands, the Army has major command bands and division bands, while the Air Force, Marine Corps, and Navy have regional bands. The Coast Guard has no regional units.

What sets the premier bands apart is that their leadership has the authority to hire musicians at a higher-than-normal beginning rank (E-6). Under normal circumstances, attainment of this rank would typically require ten to twelve years of service. Because of this pay incentive, these bands attract highly qualified musicians, making auditions very competitive.

Keep in mind that each military band has a distinct mission. Some regional bands primarily serve the base at outdoor ceremonies and parades, while others focus on performing concert tours. Since each band has its own procedures, audition requirements, and job description, it is wise to investigate the specific opportunity before spending the time, effort, and money to audition. Individuals who are interested in auditioning for a military band should contact the organization by making a phone call well in advance of the audition date.

Job Openings

As you research band job openings online, be sure to have your resume ready, as well as a cover letter and recording in case it is required. Here are some basic questions to ask a prospective military employer:

- Can you describe the military basic training experience?
- What are the job requirements?

- Will this job be mostly musical or are there other responsibilities, such as wartime tasks, to perform?
- What is the proportion of classical music as opposed to popular, show music, and functional military ceremony music performed by this band?

Military Band Audition Preparation

Military bands' websites usually contain information regarding the audition process and a number of them even provide the sheet music online. Audition repertoire normally includes one or two solo pieces such as the Mozart *Concerto*, excerpts from the band and orchestral literature, and sight-reading from the band repertoire. Some commonly listed include the following:

- Bernstein/Beeler's *Overture to Candide*
- Bizet's Intermezzo from *Carmen*, Suite No. 1
- Brahms's Symphony No. 3 in F, op. 90 (2nd movement)
- Dahl's *Sinfonietta*
- Gounod/Tobani's ballet music from *Faust*
- Grainger's *Lincolnshire Posy*
- Hindemith's Symphony in B♭
- Holst's *Hammersmith*
- Lalo/Patterson's Overture to *Le roi d'Ys*
- Makris/Bader's *Aegean Festival Overture* (cadenza)
- Mendelssohn's *A Midsummer Night's Dream* (Scherzo)
- Mozart's *Serenade No. 10* in B♭, K. 361 (6th and 7th movements)
- Suppe/Moses-Tobani's *Overture to Morning, Noon and Night in Vienna*
- Verdi/Lake's *La Forza Del Destino*

Some bands also request major, melodic minor, and harmonic minor scales extending the entire range of the instrument. Note that accurate tempo and rhythm are extremely important aspects of military band auditions, and that is it helpful to learn entire pieces rather than only excerpts.

SECRET 88: CLARINET AND ORGAN

Sooner or later, most clarinetists will be asked to play for a church service or event with the resident organist. The combination of clarinet and organ is particularly beautiful because both instruments' pipes are cylindrical, making their sounds mesh and intertwine exceptionally well, not to mention how pleasant it is to play with gorgeous church acoustics. I would like to offer suggestions for clarinet and organ repertoire, especially because very few arrangements are available transposed for B♭ instruments.

Wedding music and sacred music repertoire books/collections/online music arranged for clarinet and piano can be played with organ instead, as well as all kinds of collections of easy repertoire for clarinet and piano. When you search for albums or collections, search for words like "church," "sacred," "hymns," "worship," "encores," "faith," or "classical."

Trumpet music is another excellent source because it is usually written in B♭ and has a compatible range. Additionally, many movements from baroque sonatas for oboe also are good choices because they are easy to transpose due to their comparable range. Baroque works for flute are also suitable since they rarely include the extreme high notes found in classical or romantic flute repertoire. Some pieces from the main clarinet repertoire can also work very well, such as *Suite from the Victorian Kitchen Garden* for clarinet and harp by Paul Reade. The harp part can easily be played on organ.

Another wonderful source can be slow or *adagio* movements from various clarinet concertos and sonatas or works by composers such as Camilleri, Mangani, and the ruler of all, Mozart's Adagio from Concerto, K. 622. If you do not have an A clarinet for the Mozart Adagio, you can opt to buy an arrangement of this movement for B♭.

Famous "hits" performed on clarinet and organ include *Pie Jesu* by Fauré, *Canon* by Pachelbel, *Ave Maria* by Schubert, *Ave Verum* by Mozart, *Adagio* by Albinoni, *Wedding March* by Mendelssohn, *Ave Maria* by Gounod, *Air from Suite No. 3, Jesu, Joy of Man's Desiring*, and *Wachet Auf* chorale prelude by J. S. Bach.

It is important to note that you may want to choose an experienced organist who is able to make quick decisions regarding organ stops that are not indicated on piano parts. Also, the organist is usually knowledgeable about different religious seasons and can help you select appropriate repertoire for each one. Lastly, before committing to performing, make sure to check the organ's intonation as it can vary drastically depending on construction, temperature, and humidity. Sometimes an organ can be much flatter than A = 440 Hz. In these cases, you may have to find a longer barrel and pull it out, as well as pulling out the middle joint and bell.

Another possible solution is to play with an A clarinet with a short barrel and firm up your embouchure in order to raise the pitch. On the other hand, during hot weather the organ can be sharp, making the problem even more challenging. You may have to switch to a C clarinet and pull out all joints. Usually, the organ will be in tune, but it is wise to confirm beforehand.

SECRET 89: HISTORIC CHALUMEAU

Aside from a few baroque works, the clarinet is usually not included in early music because the instrument was invented relatively late in history. However, many baroque arrangements are available for clarinet, so it is important to study this music in order to play it in the correct style. Listening to recordings of the original instrumentation provides excellent perspective.

Jean-Luc Blasius, who teaches clarinet at Union Grand-Duc Adolphe music school (Luxembourg) and plays historic chalumeau, offers the following insight:

> The chalumeau is the ancestor of the clarinet and resembles a recorder with a single reed mouthpiece. . . . Many composers (such as Vivaldi and Graupner) loved the new instrument and started writing for it in the early eighteenth century. The most outstanding work is the concerto for two chalumeaux (alto and tenor) and orchestra by Telemann.
>
> The subsequent addition of a bell, a few keys including a register key, and most importantly, insertion of a register tube into the register key hole transformed the chalumeau into a clarinet. Copies and reconstructions of chalumeaux are built today by several makers. Fingerings are close to those of a recorder; to insure a proper chromatic scale, several half holes and forked fingerings are needed, as shown in fig. 89.1.

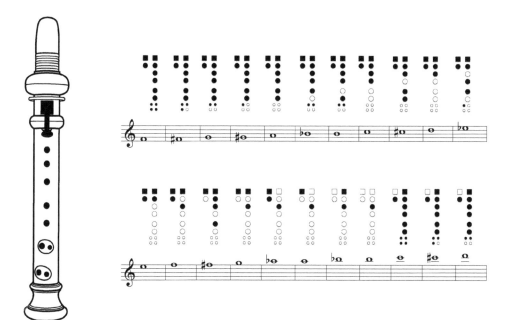

Figure 89.1

Modern clarinet reeds can be used; they might have to be clipped at the end to fit the mouthpiece, and they are tied on with a string. Historical accounts show that the chalumeau may have been played with the reed facing the upper lip, but today's players hold the reed toward the lower lip like a modern clarinet.

Playing the chalumeau is an enriching experience for any clarinetist. Not only does it open the door to a new and rich repertoire, but it is a joy to play because of the lighter air column resistance, the softness and sweetness of tone, the ease of articulation, and the opportunity to learn to perform early repertoire in the authentic style.

SECRET 90: GERMAN CLARINET

Most of us play clarinets designed with the Boehm key system (see the left side of fig. 90.1), developed in France. There was a time, however, when all classical clarinetists played the German system. Today, the German system is mainly played in Germany, Austria, parts of Switzerland, and the Netherlands (see the right side of fig 90.1). I find that getting to know this instrument offers a range of advantages for Boehm-system clarinetists.

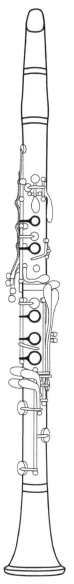
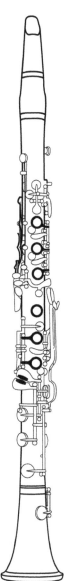

Figure 90.1

I interviewed Simone Weber, who teaches clarinet at the Luxembourg Conservatory and plays both the German and Boehm systems. She offers the following advice:

The German system is derived from Iwan Müller's thirteen-keyed clarinet from the nineteenth century and employs the same basic fingering as a chalumeau (clarinet ancestor) or recorder. Getting familiar with the German system thus enables clarinetists to learn virtually any period clarinet (baroque, classical, and romantic clarinets). It also deepens understanding of our repertoire, as many of our finest works, such as the music of Brahms, Reger, Mendelssohn, Weber, and Spohr, as well as most of the romantic orchestral literature, were written for the German clarinet.

Many fingerings, especially in the altissimo register, work on both systems but do not necessarily appear on fingering charts. Therefore, getting acquainted with a different system helps to develop the ability to choose from a variety of fingering possibilities to solve fingering challenges. Playing on instruments with different mouthpieces or bore widths will also help you become more sensitive and flexible with shaping your clarinet sound.

When trying a German clarinet for the first time, the key system might seem awkward. The tone holes are spread farther apart, some fingerings are forked (one, zero, one) and there are rollers for the little fingers to slide from one key to another instead of switching left or right. With a little practice, this can be learned quickly by using various method books such as those by Jost Michaels or Reiner Wehle.

What characterizes the German clarinet sound and soul, however, is not the fingering system. The secret lies in the larger bore, narrower mouthpiece, and smaller reed, creating a distinctive, darker sound. A typical German mouthpiece has a longer lay with a narrower tip opening, and the reed is harder and usually tied to the mouthpiece with a string ligature.

Recently, many German players have begun using non-German mouthpieces and reeds, so you might want to start with your own mouthpiece. French mouthpieces that have characteristics similar to a German-type lay include the Vandoren 5RV or M13, and barrels adapted for French mouthpieces to fit a German clarinet are available from the instrument makers.

Acquiring a German instrument is more expensive because they are still handmade. The waiting period for a clarinet ranges between one and three years, depending on the maker. Performers usually don't mind because the result is a unique, custom, exquisite-quality instrument. Compared to the Boehm-system, the German clarinet has been subject to more change throughout its history, so there are many different models on the market. Wurlitzer is one of the most established makers, and Schwenk & Seggelke, Krohntaler, and Gerold are newer makers renowned for crafting innovative instruments. Affordable options are available online from vendors such as Thomann. Note that German URLs usually end with *.de* instead of *.com*.

SECRET 91: JAZZ CLARINET

The clarinet has an important place in the history of jazz, thanks to past and present legends like Benny Goodman, Artie Shaw, Buddy DeFranco, Eddie Daniels, and Anat Cohen. Classical clarinetists can greatly enhance their musical expression by adding jazz to their training.

Although one might choose to play classical music almost exclusively, there will come a time when knowledge of the jazz style will be necessary. Perhaps a wind quintet will decide to add a jazz-style piece to their program. Since a quintet includes instruments that traditionally focus on classical repertoire (flute, oboe, bassoon, and horn), presumably the clarinetist will lead the rehearsals for this type of music. Additionally, well-known works such as George Gershwin's *Rhapsody in Blue* or Artie Shaw's *Clarinet Concerto* require clarinetists to perform in the jazz style. Saxophonist Dr. Dave Camwell of Simpson College (Iowa), offers the following advice:

> One of the most important aspects of the jazz idiom is *articulation*. While classical music primarily features on-the-beat tonguing patterns, jazz (swing, bebop) typically utilizes off-the-beat tonguing patterns. An effective way to start practicing this style is with an eight-note scale pattern (see fig. 91.1). Your tonguing should be legato. Work to apply this general articulation concept to most lines you encounter in swing-style jazz.

Jazz Off-Beat Articulation

Figure 91.1

> Another concept is note ghosting. This serves to essentially whisper certain notes in jazz phrases. Ghosting is produced by pulling the jaw slightly back from the mouthpiece while reducing the airflow or by leaving the tongue on the reed. Here is an example of how to apply ghosting to a typical line of swung eighth notes:

Figure 91.2

By using ghosting in addition to off-beat articulation, you will create a phrase that is authentic to the jazz style. As in classical music, subtlety in musical effects helps turn a good performance into a great one.

Improvisation is the core of all jazz music. With some basic skills, anyone can develop their uniquely creative musicianship in an exciting and fulfilling way. A plethora of resources on improvisation are available, which can make for an overwhelming and intimidating experience. My suggestion is to purchase the classic *Patterns for Jazz* by authors Coker, Campbell, Casale, and Greene. This book explains many theoretical concepts and, most importantly, provides extensive exercises to develop motivic ideas in all keys. This is an essential step in learning how to internalize scale/motive/key relationships in a way that is accessible to the beginner, yet progressively challenging as you develop your skills. Additionally, Jim Snidero's Jazz Conceptions website offers downloadable lessons, play-alongs, videos, and printed music. Other play-alongs, such as the Jamey Aebersold series, can also be very useful, but may be better suited to advanced players.

Additional steps to improve improvisation include transcribing your favorite melodies and solos, studying with an experienced jazz musician, and playing with others. Many colleges and adult musical organizations offer combo programs and camps that are designed for students of all ages who want to develop their musicianship in this area.

Most importantly, authentic jazz cannot be learned out of a book, so it is imperative to listen to the masters and study recordings of improvised solos. Jazz is a demanding art form, but the rewards of learning this music are worth the effort.

SECRET 92: PLAYING WORLD MUSIC

A great way to grow as a person and as an instrumentalist is to investigate un-familiar musical territory by playing world music. An interesting advantage of playing non classical music is that it can help one develop into a better and mul-tifaceted classical musician. It allows performers to acquire new techniques and become more versatile and creative, not to mention that it can eventually increase marketability as a working musician. Examples of non-classical styles include klezmer, Turkish (where the clarinet in G is the norm), Greek, Romanian, Bulgar-ian, Indian, Albanian, Latin, jazz, Dixieland, or rock.

Study

Depending on where you live and the availability of resources and venues, there are many paths that can lead to proficiency in world music. A logical first step would be to start attending live world music festivals. Not only will this expose you to various styles performed by world music bands, these events are also the perfect venues for meeting like-minded musicians. After doing a bit of research, try to find a mentor willing to either give you lessons, provide tips regarding which recordings to listen to and the appropriate literature to study, or ask if you can listen to your mentor's own group rehearse. Play along with recordings once you get comfortable with the new techniques. Playing non-classical music by ear is imperative in the long run, as most bands play without sheet music.

Forming a Band

The next step is to perform with others. Network and find musicians interested in sharing your endeavors, start working on elementary repertoire by either tran-scribing pieces from recordings or finding written material, and schedule rehears-als. Practice and discuss ways to perform each piece and find volunteers to play multiple instruments to increase tonal variety in the ensemble. Details such as special dress or attire and sound equipment can be discussed later on.

Workshops

Research music workshops or world music camps. While there might not be a clarinetist on faculty or staff, all instruments are usually welcome.

Gigs

Once your group has a one-hour set of music ready to go, try to secure performances in local parks, coffee shops, libraries, or schools. Post a website and use social media to garner interest and invitations. Naturally, the first few years will probably yield unpaid gigs, however, once you become more advanced you can start playing at local music festivals and fairs. Later on, try to attract reviewers to your concerts to improve your marketability. Bring recordings and contact information to your performances for future clients.

Recitals

One of the wonderful perks of adding any kind of non-classical music to your repertoire is performing a sample of it on your classical recitals. Audiences welcome variety, and programs ending with unusual repertoire are always warmly received.

Once your band has acquired some amount of recognition, you may wish to start commissioning composers to write for you. Depending on your situation, you may even try to write grants to fund these commissions by researching organizations that support diverse cultural ventures. Grant proposals that describe projects involving the fusion of cultures or styles such as classical-Indian or Greek-American might improve your chances of securing funding.

Playing in a world music band can be a wonderful experience musically and socially. It is a great way to learn about various cultures, languages, and a sure way to make new friends.

SECRET 93: KLEZMER

It is no secret that over the years I have concentrated a significant part of my creative efforts on performing klezmer, which is Jewish traditional celebratory music where the clarinet is typically featured as a star solo instrument. Playing klezmer allows "classical" musicians to tap into new kinds of performance venues that are less often available to them such as community gatherings, world music festivals, and Jewish ceremonies. Klezmer is made up of various modes, such as the *freygish* (Phrygian). Think of an A harmonic minor scale starting on its 5th degree (see fig. 93.1).

Figure 93.1

Although klezmer can be played on any instrument, the most traditional choices are clarinet, violin, or trumpet (for the melody parts); the harmony parts can be played on accordion, piano, guitar, or mandolin, although the mandolin is also considered a solo instrument; the rhythm section includes drums and double bass. My experience is that a small ensemble tends to sound cleaner, so I usually prefer a three-to-five-member group. A singer is a great addition to a band that plays Yiddish songs and other repertoire.

The key to learning klezmer is to listen to experts and try to assimilate the language by imitating their inflections and ornamentation. Most important is to momentarily forget what was learned during classical training and begin experimenting with a looser embouchure (with a softer reed), a flexible throat, and an idiomatic ornamental style.

Many musicians believe they must improvise, but traditional klezmer involves *ornamentation* rather than improvisation. Florid ornamentation can be regarded as a kind of improvisation, but what matters most in klezmer is to maintain a stable rhythm and keep the melody clear. After all, this is dance music and what dancers need most are a tune and a beat!

Accompanying rhythms vary according to each dance. Traditional Jewish dance is beautiful, noble, and focused on community (circle dances in a group) rather than one-on-one (person facing another) dance style. Examples of dance rhythms are the *Hora, Khosidl, Turkish, Bulgar,* and *Freylach,* as shown in fig. 93.2.

Other dances include Russian *Sher,* Romanian *Sirba,* and *Patsch Tanz.* The *Doina* is a slow, highly ornamented virtuoso piece. It is mostly non-metric and

Figure 93.2

intended for listening rather than dancing. It is usually followed by a fast dance in duple meter, such as the *Freylach* or the *Bulgar.*

Klezmer Ornamentation

Known as *dreydlekhn*, or "turns," ornaments are usually not notated. Trills and mordents are played rapidly and are used to vary repeated notes in the melody.

Bent notes, and *krechtn* (moans): *krechtn* is a general term for ornaments that imitate the sound of the break in the voice, reminiscent of the synagogue cantor chanting prayers. The *krecht* is a sudden drop of a main note. When played correctly, it sounds like "eeyack!" A *boyp* is like a *krecht* except it goes up instead of down. Also, long notes can be slightly bent here and there when the spirit moves the performer.

Glissando: glissing the pitch up and down between intervals.

Growling: playing a note while singing a dissonant note through the instrument.

Flutter tongue: rolling the tongue on a note.

Accompaniment: When other instruments are playing solos, the clarinet can accompany by improvising rhythm patterns, bass lines, arpeggiated chords, or by creating a counter melody.

To sound authentic, clarinetists need to master the art of the *krecht* (moan). A *krecht* note starts with the syllable "ee" and ends with the syllable "yak" (like a downward "chirp," ending the note with the tongue sticking on the palate *without* removing it until the sound effect is complete). The result is an extremely short and rapid downward pitch bend ending with a short "ghost" note.

Figure 93.3 is an example of a *Freylach* melody (joyful dance) followed by its ornamented version, where the *krecht* effect is illustrated as a short, downward gliss sign (bars 9–13).

Figure 93.3

Freylach Ornamented Version Instructions

In bar 1, the mordent starts with a tongue accent quickly followed by lifting the left ring finger and returning. All notes in bar 2 are slurred, but the grace notes are accented with the air column and played by *lifting the left ring finger.* Bar 3 is trilled; however, the end of the trill can be substituted with improvised technical virtuosity. Bars 4–5 include added notes to vary the original melody. In bar 7, the $a\sharp^1$ grace note is accented, and the d^3 grace note is ghosted and played with the harmonic open d^2 fingering. The half note bends down and up until bar 8. The repeated d^2 in bars 9 and 10 is played in *krechtn* (moan) style ("ee-yack"). Bar 11 is a combination of mordents and *krechtn*. In bar 18, the f^1 bends to a^1. Ghost the last note by *lifting the left ring finger very briefly,* to muffle its sound.

SECRET 94: GLISSANDO À LA GERSHWIN

Most clarinetists strive to play the opening glissando in Gershwin's *Rhapsody in Blue* as smoothly as possible. A great way to improve the technique is to practice harmonics (or partials). Play open g and, *without changing the fingering*, overblow with an air attack to produce a high d^2, followed by altissimo $b\flat^3$. Think of closing the throat gradually and move the jaw slightly forward as you go up the harmonics, resulting in the syllables "Ha," "He," and "Hee." Continue the exercise, and proceed downward in half-step increments (see fig. 94.1).

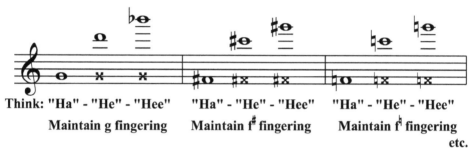

Think: "Ha" - "He" - "Hee"   "Ha" - "He" - "Hee"   "Ha" - "He" - "Hee"

Maintain g fingering   Maintain f$^\sharp$ fingering   Maintain f$^\natural$ fingering

etc.

Figure 94.1

Practice the exercise until you can play all notes back and forth as well as in random order, always using the air column instead of the tongue for each attack. Notice how your throat cavity becomes smaller as you go up the registers. For the next exercise, play open g again, and overblow to open d^2. Hold the open d^2 and try to bend the sound a half step lower to $c\sharp^2$ and slide back up to the d^2. Gradually slide up and down chromatically between each d^2, thinking of the syllables "Yee-Yah" (see fig. 94.2).

Think: "**Hee--Yah--Yee---Yah-----Yee--Yah---Yee-Yah"   etc.

*Maintain open g fingering throughout the exercise
**First note starts with "Hee" instead of "Yee"

Figure 94.2

If you are not able to maintain the d^3 without falling to the open g, play the exercise with your usual high d^2 fingering instead, until you gain control of your throat and tongue muscles more consistently.

There is a myth suggesting that an upward glissando is performed mostly with the fingers gradually sliding up the scale. Although the fingers do play a minimal part in this technique, most of the movements are executed with the throat, lips, tongue, and jaw. The fingers are most active during the low register part of a glissando and then, if performed correctly, there is a kind of "break" as you cross to the clarion register.

To illustrate this, play d¹ (fourth line on the staff), and slur up the diatonic scale to c². Then play d¹ again and lift the fingers starting at the very *tips* and uncover the holes gradually while diminishing the throat opening as you did earlier in the note-bending exercise. You will notice that soon after you lift the tips of the fingers (of both hands), the sound eventually breaks or squeaks. During that break, manipulate the shape of the throat cavity downward with the tongue so that the pitch remains flat. Open the holes gradually from the tips of the fingers and keep the pitch flat. As your fingers play an upward scale, the throat position remains in the (very open) "flat" position and gradually sharpens the pitch a step behind the fingers. With diligent practice, you will eventually adjust the lip and air pressure accordingly and work out the most efficient finger movements.

SECRET 95: VIBRATO

In new music, as well as in popular, jazz, or folk music, vibrato is an important factor in one's interpretation. There are opposing views regarding the use of vibrato in the clarinet world, and some performers prefer to dismiss the technique altogether in the context of classical music.

I believe that a very light, almost imperceptible vibrato can add color and character to a phrase from the traditional clarinet repertoire, especially within the romantic and contemporary time periods. The Hungarian melody in Kodaly's *Dances of Galanta* loses its folkloric flavor without a noticeable vibrato, and Gershwin's *Rhapsody in Blue* simply isn't the same without a jazzy vibrato.

Some schools of playing, such as the British School, tend to use vibrato more consistently than other schools. Clarinetists who generally prefer playing without vibrato can gain by adding this technique to their repertoire, if only to use it when absolutely necessary or when avant-garde composers specifically call for vibrato in their music.

Although vibrato is usually played in an even and consistent manner, it can also be played at varying speeds. A very effective way to achieve a solid and steady vibrato is to practice it very slowly at first to develop good habits right from the start. Single-reed instruments' vibrato is played with the *jaw*. Four factors make a good vibrato:

1. Shape—the actual contour, roundness, and shape of each wave
2. Control—the evenness of each wave
3. Speed—the number of waves during a specific amount of time
4. Consistency—the uniformity of each wave on long notes

Shape

Play a long tone on open g for a few seconds. While imagining and articulating the syllables "Wow-Wow-Wow," slowly and gradually lower your jaw (this will make the pitch go down). Slowly move the jaw back up toward the reed and repeat both motions several times, making sure the jaw moves continuously without interruptions in the sound. Coming back up with the jaw at the end of each wave prevents sawtooth wave shapes. The jaw moves 50 percent down, 50 percent up, always coming back to the starting position in the middle. Try different depths of undulations to vary the vibrato's character. Do *not* execute vibrato with the diaphragm or throat.

Figure 95.1

Control

Once you master the roundness of each wave with the jaw, use the metronome at a very slow speed, and play four beats "straight" (no vibrato), followed by four beats with "vibrato quarter notes" (one evenly shaped wave per beat):

Figure 95.2

Speed

With the metronome at a low speed, play a whole note, then vibrate at two half notes, four quarter notes, eight eighth notes, four eighth-note triplets (resulting in twelve notes), and 16 sixteenth notes. Keep the tempo steady, and gradually increase the speed at the start of each new set. (Think: "wow," "wow-wow," "wow-wow-wow-wow" until you reach the tempo ♩ = 84.)

Figure 95.3

Consistency

To stabilize the jaw, play a whole note, followed by four beats of four sixteenth notes, and alternate back and forth. Make sure all waves are even.

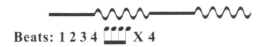

Figure 95.4

SECRET 96: CIRCULAR BREATHING

Circular breathing is a fun, but challenging, technique that allows wind players to play for extended periods without interruption. This is achieved by producing a continuous sound by using the cheeks as an air reservoir and breathing through the nose while the stored air is forced from the mouth into the instrument. In traditional repertoire, it is almost always possible to find a place to breathe, although some long virtuoso passages could be played with this technique. Circular breathing also produces spectacular effects in contemporary music.

A good way to master this challenging task is to practice spitting water in a steady stream while inhaling through the nose simultaneously. The cheek and tongue muscles control the output of the water while the lungs inhale through the nose. To apply this to a wind instrument, it is necessary to develop a series of abilities beforehand. First, gather the following items:

1 plastic coffee stirrer (with two small tubes)
1 small drinking straw
1 large glass of water
1 kitchen sink (or a back yard)
1 clarinet
1 healthy dose of perseverance

First, it is important to understand which muscles will be doing most of the work. The first muscles to train are the tongue, cheek, and throat muscles. These muscles will be working independently from the lungs, so it is crucial to learn how to move them separately. With the tongue, close the throat (as in the last part of the word "gig") and breathe in and out through the nose several times. This is easy! Then, still breathing from the nose, open the mouth and move the tongue in various directions while inhaling and exhaling. Still easy.

The next muscles to be aware of are the cheek muscles that act as an air compressor to control the airflow. Take as much water as possible in your mouth, then close the throat and puff your water-filled cheeks. Hold the coffee stirrer between your lips. Over a sink (or outdoors), push the water out of the stirrer, creating a strong and even flow with your cheeks and tongue. The water should come out as a straight long spurt with no interruption. The stronger the muscles contract, the less chance the water will slow down and drip down the chin. This water flow simulates what will later become the airflow in your instrument while you breathe, so try breathing in and out as the water flows out.

Try the same exercise with a small and narrow drinking straw. The straw's opening offers less resistance than the stirrer and emulates clarinet playing more realistically. Then, remove the straw and do the same exercise with the lips *only*, spitting water in a straight long line, while inhaling.

After gaining control of the cheek and tongue muscles, play a note through the mouthpiece and barrel *only*. The idea is to play a note *without* using air from the lungs. While closing your throat and forming your embouchure, puff the cheeks and try squeezing air into the mouthpiece. Remember to close your throat so that you won't be tempted to use the air column. At first, it might seem virtually impossible to create a sound using only the air stored in your cheeks. Imagine pronouncing the letter "p" in a popping manner. Compress the air in the cheeks while almost blocking the air from the mouthpiece opening with the lips, and then free the opening so that the air is forced in the instrument to create a rather harsh and unattractive tone, but a tone nevertheless. In time, the notes should become longer. Later, do this exercise with the entire instrument (low notes are easier).

You are now ready to combine all movements. While playing and sustaining a low note, gradually puff your cheeks until they are full of air. Close the throat and push the air into the instrument with your cheeks and tongue, as you did earlier with the water and straw. While you empty your cheeks, inhale through the nose. Gently restore the natural airflow by slowly and gradually reopening the throat without creating a "bump" caused by quickly forcing the air out of the lungs.

After practicing circular long tones, try with various scales and trills. It is wise to choose to circular breathe during technical passages to camouflage any imperfections. Some instruments where the air column resistance is naturally greater (e.g., oboe) make this technique more feasible, whereas instruments with low resistance (flute, clarinet) demand more cheek control and practice. A good preparatory exercise is to practice blowing constant bubbles in a glass of water with the stirrer, followed by the straw, while spitting water before attempting it with the clarinet. In time, the movements should be done more quickly and smoothly, with nearly imperceptible puffing of the cheeks.

SECRET 97: MULTIPHONICS

The clarinet is a monophonic instrument. However, multiple sounds can be created with a technique called multiphonics. Clarinetists often play multiphonics without even knowing it when their sound inadvertently cracks or splits into two separate harmonics. The valuable part is learning to control it.

New music specialist Dr. Gregory Oakes, associate professor of clarinet at Iowa State University, offers this advice:

> There are two ways to create multiphonics:
>
> *One—with a change in the shape of the oral cavity.* For example, while playing high a^1 and purposefully lowering the middle part of the tongue (like saying "ah"), the f (first space) will sound simultaneously. Experiment with dropping the tongue position far enough so that the a^1 disappears and only the f remains. The tone will be fuzzy and unfocused. Gradually raise that tongue to hear the a^1 reappear. If you were to continue raising the tongue to its highest position (like saying "ee"), the lower note would disappear entirely, which is the standard technique for playing a single high note that we normally use. This multiphonic appears in Helmut Lachenmann's solo clarinet piece, *Dal Niente*.

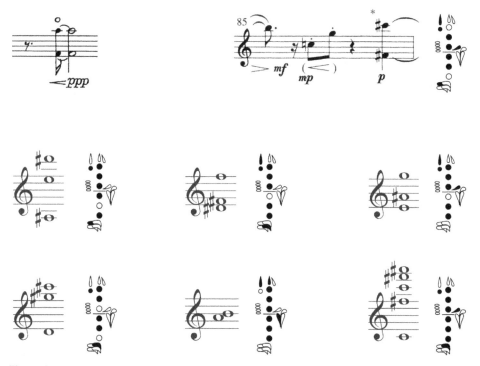

Figure 97.1

Two—with special fingerings (usually already written into the part). It is important to note, however, that adjustments to the oral cavity are still an essential part
of making any multiphonic speak well. One good example is the multiphonic from
the last page of Elliott Carter's *Gra*. Using the provided fingering, many clarinetists
can make it speak with only slight variation of the oral cavity. Figure 97.1 shows
six different multiphonics fingerings. Try each one to see how they differ in sound
as well as the oral cavity adjustments necessary to create them. Some will be quite
free-blowing while others will be more resistant. Getting a sense of how each one
feels is the secret to making them work.

SECRET 98: GROWLING

Growling is a technique that can add a wonderful effect in jazz, klezmer, and pop music. Growling results from singing a note into the clarinet while simultaneously playing, and its intensity depends on the amount of dissonance created by the two different notes.

Learning to sing while playing can be tricky because players are used to blowing through the bore without vibrating the vocal cords. I recommend singing through the clarinet *without* playing at first. Sing loudly through the bore and wait until the reed starts creating a sound simultaneously.

Another helpful preliminary exercise is to whistle a note and sing a note at the same time. You can also practice singing while blowing air into the palm of your hand or through a drinking straw.

Although growling is most effective in the upper register, it is easiest to practice it in the lower register at first. Play a low note and simultaneously sing the note a fifth above. For example, if your voice range allows, play a low E while singing the B above it. If one or both notes do not come out, try singing the B through the bore without playing. Then increase your singing volume and airflow until the low E comes out. Experiment with singing different notes against the note you are playing. Play a long tone while glissing up and down with your voice through the bore.

Once you have achieved initial success, it is important to balance the voice and the clarinet volumes. Record yourself to verify evenness and determine which notes produce the best growl. One problem is that sometimes beginners tend to overuse the growling effect, which may cause some throat irritation.

An excellent resource to practice singing while playing is Ronald L. Caravan's *Preliminary Exercises and Etudes in Contemporary Techniques for Clarinet*, published by Ethos. The book contains preliminary exercises such as *Matching Pitches, Scales with Pedal, Scales in Parallel Thirds, Scales in Thirds in Canonic Pattern, Intervals,* and *Melodic Leaps*.

Other interesting applications with singing are as follows:

1. Play parallel intervals.
2. Play melodic lines with accompaniment (see fig. 98.1, A); alternate clarinet and voice lines as the melody.
3. Move the voice line against a nonmoving clarinet note, and vice versa (A).
4. Play a canon such as *Frère Jacques* with both your clarinet and your voice (B).

Ex. A

Frère Jacques

Ex. B

Figure 98.1

SECRET 99: BRAVING STAGE FRIGHT

Clarinet teachers hear it so many times from students: "But I sounded so much better in the practice room!" It occurred to me that students prepare their weekly lessons alone in the practice room for *six* days while they perform their lesson in front of a teacher or student group only *one* day each week. Somehow, musicians seem to expect to deliver a perfect performance in front of an audience even though they spent most of their time preparing in a vacant room. Consequently, practicing alone in a cubicle does not adequately prepare us for performing. Stage fright (or performance anxiety) can arise days, or even weeks, before the actual event. Some symptoms include a fast heart rate, shaking hands, dry mouth, memory blanks, or digestive problems. It can afflict amateur musicians as well as world-renowned artists and can vary in severity.

One obvious difference between practicing and performing is that we become more self-aware when people are present compared to when we are alone. A quick exercise to test this theory would be to see how your concentration is affected if you leave the practice room door open, when more people might hear you practice.

When we practice hour after hour, we enter a zone in which musical concentration is paramount. Our self-awareness seems to disappear and all of our attention is focused on correct fingerings, note attacks, tone nuances, and rhythm. As soon as listeners are present, we suddenly move out of that zone and become more aware of our bodies to the point of forgetting simple things such as fingerings. Each movement becomes a chore, panic sets in, and the performance is compromised. The tips that follow will help you to reduce the effects of stage fright:

1. Greet audience members as they enter the recital hall to make the experience less formal and to help you feel that you are performing for friends rather than strangers.
2. Project assertiveness and a positive attitude on stage to relax listeners and enhance their overall response.
3. Talk to the audience between pieces. This helps diminish stress and transforms the event into an interactive experience rather than placing all the weight on the performer's shoulders.
4. Choose a concert outfit that makes you feel professional and confident.
5. Perform as much as possible so that you can eventually turn a stressful situation into a simple day-to-day "this is my job" kind of affair.
6. Attend other recitals. Invariably, you will find that you are mostly concentrating on listening to the music rather than finding each and every flaw. Realizing this will help you remember that the same will be true during your own performance.

7. Practice random spots in your music to see if you can play error-free on the first try, just as you aim to do during a performance.

8. Be self-aware as you practice. Visualize the concert hall, the audience, the stage spotlights, and overall ambiance of the evening.

9. Practice with accompaniment as often as possible. This helps you to focus on things other than your solo part and simulates a live performance situation.

10. Record your practice sessions. An interesting exercise is to turn on a recording or video device, leave the room, and reenter as if a listener is waiting for you.

11. Memorize your program. Even though you may decide to perform with your music, memorization can give you an array of backup tools in moments of stress.

12. Prepare a series of concert-quality reeds. Knowing that you have reliable reeds will inevitably reduce your stress level.

13. Listen to your most successful past performances. This is a terrific way to build confidence and to gather clues about what you do best as a musician.

14. Save your lip. It is important not to practice to the point of tiring your embouchure on the day of a performance.

SECRET 100: TECHNOLOGY FOR CLARINETISTS

Technology enables wind players to expand their musical palette in exciting ways.

Microphone

The first item to acquire is a microphone to amplify your instrument. This can be achieved with a freestanding microphone or a microphone that is attached to the clarinet. Models of the latter vary in capability and price but because the clarinet tone exits the bore from the tone holes as well as the bell, I suggest buying a model with two microphone extensions, often called a "double gooseneck." Products made by Applied Microphone Technology are highly recommended. Some models are wireless, which allows for untethered movement on stage.

Guitar Pedals

To start experimenting with simple machines, use guitar pedals to electronically manipulate your clarinet sound. Some effective devices for wind instruments include the Octaver (plays an octave below), the Digital Sampler/Delay (records notes for sampling and plays notes with delay and echo effects), and the Flange (distorts the sound). Connect the output of your microphone to the input of the pedal(s), and connect them to an amplifier. Play with all the pedals together or turn some of them off to create different sounds.

SmartMusic

SmartMusic is a very popular interactive virtual piano accompaniment system and a fantastic practice and teaching tool. You can slow down clarinet accompaniments (available through an online subscription), loop difficult passages, record and e-mail files, and have it follow expressive tempo changes. There are technical and sight-reading exercises, in any key and tempo, with onscreen assessment. Custom accompaniments can also be created with the music notation program Finale.

EWI (Electronic Wind Instrument)

Keyboard players play synthesizers in contemporary, popular, or rock music. Thanks to inventors like Nyle Steiner, clarinetists can express themselves with MIDI language by using wind to control synthesizers and other devices, thereby creating a lyrical dimension to electronic music.

Before trying any device, the first step toward performing with sound processors is to learn about electronic music. Read about it, take an introductory course, meet specialists, and talk with knowledgeable sales representatives. The more you know, the better you prepare yourself to adequately tackle synthesized music.

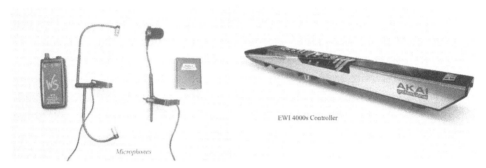

EWI 4000s Controller

Microphones

Figure 100.1

The acronym MIDI stands for Musical Instrument Digital Interface, which allows electronic instruments to communicate with each other. The EWI (Electronic Wind Instrument) can play a very large range, transpose, bend notes, play polyphonically, and sound like any imaginable instrument. The EWI is expressive because it is "touch sensitive," so notes are changed simply by touching the metal keys, and its air pressure sensor allows it to play an array of dynamics, as well as vibrato, very much like a woodwind instrument.

Electronic devices become obsolete so quickly that it is impractical to recommend specific models.

QUICK-TIPS BULLETIN BOARD—FINAL TIPS

- Learn to sing. Singing is a great way to conceptualize wind control more clearly and improve listening skills.
- When practicing technical passages, learn to see the big picture as well as details. Instead of focusing solely on technical challenges within a musical phrase, take a "step back to see the forest for the trees" and envision the over-all phrase's line and direction.
- During rehearsals, show professionalism by paying close attention to the instructions given to the ensemble and, above all, resist infamous habits such as reading, talking, or texting while sitting through extended rests or *tacet* movements.
- Listen to live concerts and recordings of master musicians. Listening to great performers is a lesson in itself, especially when you listen to your favorites on a regular basis. The more you listen, the more details become apparent, which in turn can be imitated more easily.
- Embrace technology. Musicians need to remember that technology impacts their work significantly on a daily basis. Musicians self-produce professional-quality videos and recordings, create promotional websites, and advertise and teach online. Having the vision to use technology to help further your career is essential.
- Join the International Clarinet Association (ICA), which offers a quarterly subscription to a stellar clarinet magazine called *The Clarinet*. The ICA is an organization that meets in various locations within the United States and around the world for an annual event called ClarinetFest. It supports an ex-tensive research library with materials available to all members and promotes a variety of endeavors related to clarinet such as performance, research, and composition competitions.
- Read as much as you can about your instrument.

Further Reading

CHAPTERS 1–3: TONGUING, INTONATION, AND TONE STRATEGIES

Brymer, Jack. *Clarinet*. London: Kahn and Averill, 1976.

Paglialonga, Phillip O. *Squeak Big: Practical Fundamentals for the Successful Clarinetist*. Medina, NY: Imagine Music, 2015.

Stein, Keith. *The Art of Clarinet Playing*. Princeton: Summy-Birchard, 1958.

CHAPTER 4: TECHNICAL STRATEGIES

Scales and Rhythm

Johnston, Philip. *Rhythm Bootcamp: The Fastest, Most Addictive Way to Level Up Your Rhythm Reading*. n.p.: Philip Johnston, 2014.

———. *Scales Bootcamp: The Fastest, Clearest Way to Get to Know Your Scales, and Then Master Them*. n.p.: InsideMusicTeaching, 2009.

Altissimo

Drushler, Paul. *The Altissimo Register: A Partial Approach*. Rochester, NY: Shall-u-mo Publications, 1978.

Ridenour, Tom. *The Annotated Book of Altissimo Clarinet Fingerings: An Invaluable Workbook and Guide for the Serious Clarinetist*. Orlando, FL: Tom's Clarinet Service, 1986.

Sim, Alan C. *Clarinet Fingerings*. Stebbing, Essex: Twydds Music, 1991.

CHAPTER 5: MUSICIANSHIP STRATEGIES

Practice Tactics

Bruser, Madeline. *The Art of Practicing: A Guide to Making Music from the Heart.* With a foreword by Yehudi Menuhin. New York: Bell Tower, 1999.

Chesebro, Robert, and Kelvin Tod Kerstetter. *The Everyday Virtuoso: A Structured Approach to Developing Technique for Collegiate and Advanced High School Clarinetists.* Bloomington, IN: Woodwindiana, 2008.

Dumais, David. *Music Practice: The Musician's Guide to Practicing and Mastering Your Instrument Like a Professional.* n.p.: CreateSpace Independent Publishing Platform, 2015. Kindle Edition.

Heany, Tom. *First, Learn to Practice.* Indianapolis: Dog Ear Publishing, 2012.

Harnum, Jonathan. *The Practice of Practice: How to Boost Your Music Skills.* Chicago: Sol-Ut Press, 2014.

Ingkavet, Andrew. *The Game of Practice: With 53 Tips to Make Practice Fun!* New York: Musicolor Method, 2016. Kindle Edition.

Johnston, Philip. *The Practice Revolution: Getting Great Results from the Six Days Between Music Lessons.* PearceAustralia: PracticeSpot Press, 2002.

———. *Practiceopedia: The Musician's Illustrated Guide to Practicing.* Pearce, Australia: PracticeSpot Press, 2006.

Snitkin, Harvey R. *Practicing for Young Musicians: You Are Your Own Teacher.* Niantic, CT: HMS Publications, 1997.

Practice Journals

Faber, Nancy, Randall Faber, Carolyn Inabinet, and Paula Peterson-Heil. *Practice and Progress Lesson Notebook*: *Assignment and Evaluation Record.* North Miami Beach, FL: FJH Music Co., 1989.

Hal Leonard Corporation. *Musician's Practice Planner: A Weekly Lesson Planner for Music Students.* Oakland, CA: Molto Music Publishing Company, 1999.

Incredibly Useful Notebooks. *Musician's Practice Journal: Practicing Log and Music Planner for All Musicians.* n.p.: Fuller Street Music and Media, 2015.

Kaplan, Burton. *The Musician's Practice Log.* New York: Perception Development Techniques, 1985.

Snitkin, Harvey. *Practice Planner: A Journal of Goals and Progress.* Niantic, CT: HMS Publications, 2002.

Playing Posture

Bond, Mary. *The New Rules of Posture: How to Sit, Stand, and Move in the Modern World.* Rochester, VT: Healing Arts Press, 2007.

CHAPTER 6: REEDS AND EQUIPMENT

Instrument Selection

Pinksterboer, Hugo. *Tipbook Clarinet: The Complete Guide*. 2nd ed. Milwaukee: Hal Leonard Books, 2010.

Reeds

Guy, Larry. *Selection, Adjustment, and Care of Single Reeds: A Handbook for Clarinetists and Saxophonists with Guidelines for Selecting and Breaking in Reeds to Achieve the Best Results*. 3rd ed. Stony Point, NY: Rico Editions by D'Addario, 2012.

Karlsson, Heather. *Care and Feeding of Your Clarinet: A User's Guide to Basic Maintenance*. Carrollton, TX: H. Karlsson Woodwinds, 2008.

Ormand, Fred. *The Single Reed Adjustment Manual*. Las Vegas: Amilcare Publications, 2000.

CHAPTER 7: ENHANCING REPERTOIRE

Orchestral Performance and Excerpts

Atkins, Dave. "Tips for Freelancers." In *Selected Clarinet Masterclasses*, edited by the editors of *Windplayer*. Malibu, CA: Windplayer Publications, 1998.

Davis, Richard. *Becoming an Orchestral Musician: A Guide for Aspiring Professionals*. London: Giles de la Mare, 2004.

Hadcock, Peter. *The Working Clarinetist: Master Classes with Peter Hadcock*. Edited by Bruce Ronkin, Aline Benoit, and Marshall Burlingame. Cherry Hill, NJ: Roncorp, Inc., 1999.

Hepp, Heinz, and Albert Rohde. *Orchester Probespiel: Test Pieces for Orchestral Auditions for Clarinet*. Frankfurt and London: C.F. Peters, 1991.

McGinnis, Robert, and Stanley Drucker. *Orchestral Excerpts from the Symphonic Repertoire for Clarinet: Classical and Modern Works*. 8 vols. New York: International Music, 1950–1992.

Merrer, Jacques. *Orchestral Excerpts for Sopranino Clarinet*. 10 vols. Paris: International Music Diffusion, 2001–2015.

The Orchestral Musician's CD-Rom Library: Clarinet. 12 vols. United States: CD Sheet Music, LLC, distributed by Hal Leonard Corp., 2003–2009. CD-ROM.

Strauss, Richard. *Orchestral Excerpts from Symphonic Works for Clarinet*. 3 vols. Edited by Franz Bartholomey. New York: International Music, n.d.

Bass Clarinet

Arnold, Martin. *Bass Clarinet Scale Book*. 2nd ed. Toronto: Aztecpress, 2003.

Bona, Pasquale. *Rhythmical Articulation Studies for Bass Clef Instruments*. Selected and transcribed by William D. Fitch. New York: Carl Fischer, 1969.

Rhoads, William E., ed. *18 Selected Etudes for Alto and Bass Clarinet*. San Antonio: Southern Music Company, 1963.

————. *21 Foundation Studies for Alto and Bass Clarinet*. San Antonio: Southern Music, 1965.

————. *35 Technical Studies for Alto and Bass Clarinet*. San Antonio: Southern Music, 1962.

Rubio, Pedro. *Studies for Bass Clarinet*. 2 vols. Madrid: Música Didáctica, 2004–2006.

Sparnaay, Harry. *The Bass Clarinet: A Personal History*. Translated by Annelie de Man and Paul Roe. 3rd ed. Barcelona, Spain: Periferia Sheet Music, 2011.

Volta, Jean-Marc. *The Bass Clarinet*. Paris: International Music Diffusion, 1996.

Watts, Sarah. *Spectral Immersions: A Comprehensive Guide to the Theory and Practice of Bass Clarinet Multiphonics*. Ruisbroek-Puurs: Metropolis, 2015.

Weissenborn, Julius. *Advanced Studies from the Works of Julius Weissenborn: Adapted for Alto and Bass Clarinets*. Arranged by William E. Rhoads. San Antonio: Southern Music Company, 1973.

Woodwind Doubling

Jeanjean, Paul. *"Vade-Mecum" of the Clarinet-Player: Six Special Studies to Render the Fingers and Tongue Rapidly Supple*. Paris: A. Leduc, 1927.

Moyse, Marcel. *On Sonority: Art and Technique*. Paris: A. Leduc, 1934.

Rascher, Sigurd. *Top-Tones for the Saxophone*. 3rd ed. New York: Carl Fischer, 1977.

Ronkin, Bruce, and Robert Frascotti. *The Orchestral Saxophonist*. 2 vols. Cherry Hill, NJ: Roncorp, 1978.

Clarinet, Organ, and Sacred Repertoire

Christopher, Keith. *Great Is the Lord*. Milwaukee: Hal Leonard, 2003.

Drucker, Stanley, arranger. *Album of Classical Pieces for Clarinet and Piano*. 2 vols. New York: International Music Company, 1954.

Heim, Norman. *Sacred Melodies for Clarinet Solo with Keyboard Accompaniment*. Pacific, MO: Mel Bay Publications, 1988.

Holcombe, Bill. *Songs of Faith: For Trumpet and Piano*. 2 vols. West Trenton, NJ: Musicians Publications, 1992.

Hölÿ, Fritz-Georg, and Otmar Mayer, arrangers. *Encores and Pieces for Clarinet and Organ*. Lottstetten and Adliswil: A. J. Kunzelmann, 2002.

Pethel, Stan. *Sounds of Worship: Solos with Ensemble Arrangements for Two or More Players*. Milwaukee: Brookfield Press, 2004.

Jazz Clarinet

Aebersold, Jamey. *Jamey Aebersold Play-A-Long Series*. 133 vols. New Albany, IN: Jamey Aebersold Jazz, 1992–2012.

Coker, Jerry, Jimmy Casale, Gary Campbell, and Jerry Greene. *Patterns for Jazz*. 3rd ed. Lebanon, IN: Studio P/R, 1970.

Firestone, Ross. *Swing, Swing, Swing: The Life and Times of Benny Goodman*. New York: Norton, 1993.

Snidero, Jim. *Easy Jazz Conception for Clarinet*. Rottenburg: Advance Music, 2000.

———. *Intermediate Jazz Conception for Clarinet*. Rottenburg: Advance Music, 2005.

———. *Jazz Conception: 21 Solo Etudes for Jazz Phrasing, Interpretation, and Improvisation for Clarinet*. Mainz, Germany: Advance Music, 1996.

Zammarchi, Fabrice, and Sylvie Mas. *A Life in the Golden Age of Jazz: A Bibliography of Buddy DeFranco*. Seattle: Parkside, 2002.

Klezmer Clarinet

Bock, Jerry, Sheldon Harnick, and Carol Cuellar. *Selections from Fiddler on the Roof: Clarinet*. Arranged by David Pugh. Miami: Warner Bros., 1995.

Card, Patricia Pierce. "The Influence of Klezmer on Twentieth-Century Solo and Chamber Concert Music for Clarinet: With Three Recitals of Selected Works of Manevich, Debussy, Horovitz, Mihaud, Martino, Mozart, and Others." D.M.A. diss., University of North Texas, 2002. http://digital.library.unt.edu/ark:/67531/metadc3355/m1/1/.

Ciesla, Alexis, and Bastienne Lapalud. *Five Klezmer Pieces for Clarinet and Piano*. Tübingen, Germany: Advance Music, 2007.

Curtis, Mike. *Ten Klezmer Duos for Two B-Flat Clarinets*. 2 vols. Rottenburg: Advance Music, 2007.

Flato, Jud. *The Ultimate "Little Big Band": All-Time Jewish Hits for Clarinet*. United States: Tara Publications, 2005.

Galay, Daniel. *Klezmer Tunes with a Classical Touch: For Violin or Clarinet with Piano Accompaniment*. Kfar Sava, Israel: Or-Tav Music Publications, 1998.

Jones, Edward Huws, and Gillian Shepherd. *The Klezmer Clarinet: Jewish Music of Celebration*. London: Boosey and Hawkes, 2002.

Kammen, Jack, and Joseph Kammen. *Kammen International Dance Folio No. 1: Big Collection of Carefully Selected International Songs and Dances, Good for All Occasions for Clarinet or Tenor Sax*. New York: J. and J. Kammen Music Co., 1924.

———. *Kammen International Dance and Concert Folio No. 9: A Collection of Famous International Songs, Dances, Medleys, Selections, and Overture for Clarinet or Tenor Sax*. New York: J. and J. Kammen Music Co., 1934.

Phillips, Stacy. *Easy Klezmer Tunes*. Pacific, MO: Mel Bay Publications, 2003.

Przystaniak, Peter, and Irith Gabriely. *That's Klezmer: 12 pieces for 1 or 2 Clarinets and Piano*. Frankfurt and New York: H. Litolff and C. F. Peters, 2008.

Richmond, Ken, and Yale Klezmer Band. *The Klezmer Band B-Flat Folio*. Cedarhurst, NY: Tara Publications, 1997.

Rosenberg, Marvin. *Dance Klezmer Style!* Cedarhurst, NY: Tara Publications, 1995.

Strom, Yale. *Dave Tarras, the King of Klezmer*. Kfar Sara: Or-Tav Music Publications, 2010.

————. *World Music: Klezmer Play-Along Clarinet*. Vienna and New York: Universal Edition, 2008.

Wolfgram, Coen. *Klezmers for B-Flat Clarinet and Piano Accompaniment*. Heerenveen, Holland: DeHaske. Distributed by Hal Leonard, 1997.

Extended Techniques

Caravan, Ronald L. *Preliminary Exercises and Etudes in Contemporary Techniques for Clarinet: Introductory Material for the Study of Multiphonics, Quarter Tones, and Timbre Variation*. Oswego, NY: Ethos Publications, 1979.

Rehfeldt, Phillip. *New Directions for Clarinet*. 2nd ed. Lanham, MD: Scarecrow Press, 2003.

Spring, Robert. *Circular Breathing: A Method*. Malibu, CA: Windplayer Publications, 2006.

OTHER IMPORTANT TOPICS

Acoustics

Benade, Arthur H. *Fundamentals of Musical Acoustics*. 2nd ed. New York: Dover Publications, Inc., 1990.

Career Success

Bartiromo, Maria. *The 10 Laws of Enduring Success*. With Catherine Whitney. New York: Crown Business, 2010.

Beeching, Angela Myles. *Beyond Talent: Creating a Successful Career in Music*. Oxford: Oxford University Press, 2010.

Bird, Polly. *Improve Your Time Management*. Blacklick, OH: McGraw-Hill, 2010.

Bixler, Susan, and Lisa Scherrer Dugan. *5 Steps to Professional Presence: How to Project Confidence, Competence, and Credibility at Work*. Holbrook, MA: Adams Media Corp., 2001.

Carlson, Richard. *Don't Sweat the Small Stuff . . . and It's All Small Stuff: Simple Ways to Keep the Little Things from Taking Over Your Life*. New York: Hyperion, 1997.

————. *Don't Sweat the Small Stuff at Work: Simple Ways to Minimize Stress and Conflict While Bringing Out the Best in Yourself and Others*. New York: Hyperion, 1998.

Carnegie, Dale. *How to Win Friends and Influence People*. Edited by Dorothy Carnegie and Arthur R. Pell. New York: Simon and Schuster, 1981.

Cutler, David. *The Savvy Musician: Building a Career, Earning a Living, and Making a Difference*. Pittsburgh: Helius Press, 2010.

Frankel, Lois P. *Nice Girls Don't Get the Corner Office: 101 Unconscious Mistakes Women Make That Sabotage Their Careers*. New York: Warner Business Books, 2004.

Gladwell, Malcolm. *Outliers: The Story of Success.* New York: Little, Brown, and Co., 2008.

Godin, Seth. *Purple Cow: Transform Your Business by Being Remarkable.* New York: Portfolio, 2003.

Johnson, Spencer. *Who Moved My Cheese? An Amazing Way to Deal with Change in Your Work and in Your Life.* New York: Putnam, 1998.

Kelley, Robert Earl. *How to Be a Star at Work: Nine Breakthrough Strategies You Need to Succeed.* New York: Times Business, 1998.

Pink, Daniel H. *A Whole New Mind: Why Right-Brainers Will Rule the Future.* New York: Riverhead Books, 2006.

Popyk, Bob. *The Business of Getting More Gigs as a Professional Musician.* Milwaukee: Hal Leonard Corp., 2003.

Rosenberg, Arthur D. *101 Ways to Stand Out at Work: How to Get the Recognition and Rewards You Deserve.* Cincinnati: Adams Media, 2010.

Schonberg, Alan R., Robert L. Shook, and Donna Estreicher. *169 Ways to Score Points with Your Boss.* Lincolnwood, IL: Contemporary Books, 1998.

Shepard, Glenn. *How to Be the Employee Your Company Can't Live Without: 18 Ways to Become Indispensable.* Hoboken, NJ: John Wiley, 2006.

Weber, Eric. *The Indispensable Employee.* Toronto: Coles, 1980.

Whitten, Neal. *Becoming an Indispensable Employee in a Disposable World.* Amsterdam and San Diego: Pfeiffer, 1995.

Financial Management

Chatzky, Jean Sherman. *Pay It Down! From Debt to Wealth on $10 a Day.* New York: Portfolio: 2004.

Dahl, Jonathan. *1,001 Things They Won't Tell You: An Insider's Guide to Spending, Saving, and Living Wisely.* New York: Workman Pub. Co., 2009.

Davidoff, Howard. *The Everything Personal Finance in Your 20s and 30s Book: Erase Your Debt, Personalize Your Budget, and Plan Now to Secure Your Future.* 2nd ed. Avon, MA: Adams Media Corp., 2008.

Fisher, Sarah Young, and Susan Shelly. *The Complete Idiot's Guide to Personal Finance in Your 20s and 30s.* 3rd ed. Indianapolis: Alpha, 2005.

Gaines, Pam, and Cathy McCormack. *Financial Management for Musicians.* Edited by Rick Weldon. Emeryville, CA: MixBooks by Intertec Publishing; Milwaukee: distributed by Hal Leonard, 1999.

Orman, Suze. *The Money Book for the Young, Fabulous, and Broke.* New York: Riverhead Books, 2005.

Siteman, Michelle. *The Pleasures and Perils of Raising Young Musicians: A Guide for Parents.* Bloomington, IN: Author House, 2007.

Tyson, Eric. *Personal Finance for Dummies.* 8th ed. Hoboken, NJ: John and Wiley and Sons, Inc., 2016.

Scholarship

Gee, Harry R. *Clarinet Solo de Concours, 1897–1980: An Annotated Bibliography*. Bloomington, IN: Indiana University Press, 1981.

Hoeprich, Eric. *The Clarinet*. New Haven and London: Yale University Press, 2008.

Lawson, Colin. *The Cambridge Companion to the Clarinet*. New York: Cambridge University Press, 1995.

Stage Presence and Performance Anxiety

Gordon, Stewart. *Mastering the Art of Performance: A Primer for Musicians*. New York: Oxford University Press, 2006.

Greene, Don. *Performance Success: Performing Your Best under Pressure*. New York: Routledge, 2002.

Hagberg, Karen A. *Stage Presence from Head to Toe: A Manual for Musicians*. Lanham, MD: Scarecrow Press, 2003.

Jones, Kate. *Keeping Your Nerve! Confidence Boosting Strategies for Musicians and Performers*. London: Faber Music, 2000.

Teaching Studios

Johnston, Philip. *The Dynamic Studio: How to Keep Students, Dazzle Parents, and Build the Music Studio Everyone Wants to Get Into*. n.p.: InsideMusicTeaching, 2012.

———. *The Practice Spot Guide to Promoting Your Teaching Studio: How to Make Your Phone Ring, Fill Your Schedule, and Build a Waiting List You Can't Jump Over*. Pearce, Australia: PracticeSpot Press, 2003.

Wellness

Andrews, Elizabeth. *Muscle Management for Musicians*. Lanham, MD: Scarecrow Press, 2005.

Dawson, William J. *Fit as a Fiddle: The Musician's Guide to Playing Healthy*. Lanham: Rowman & Littlefield Education, 2008.

Horvath, Janet. *Playing (Less) Hurt: An Injury Prevention Guide for Musicians*. New York: Hal Leonard Books, 2010.

Klickstein, Gerald. *The Musician's Way: A Guide to Practice, Performance, and Wellness*. Oxford and New York: Oxford University Press, 2009.

Liebermann, Julie Lyonn. *You Are Your Instrument: The Definitive Musician's Guide to Practice and Performance*. New York: Huiksi Music, 1991.

Norris, Richard. *The Musician's Survival Manual: A Guide to Preventing and Treating Injuries in Instrumentalists*. Saint Louis: M. M. B. Music, 1993.

Paull, Barbara, and Christine Harrison. *The Athletic Musician: A Guide to Playing without Pain*. Lanham: Scarecrow Press, 1997.

Pollan, Michael. *Food Rules: An Eater's Manual*. New York: Penguin Books, 2009.

Index

Müller, 168
multiphonics, 183–84, 196, 198

nature, 103–4, 107
neck, 12, 111, 115, 157
neck-strap, 136–37

Oakes, Greg, xiii, 183
opera arias, 107–8
orchestral excerpts, 2, 20, 58, 93, 158, 195
organ, 164, 196

Paglialonga, Phillip O., xiii, 65, 193
pain, 136, 200
Palanker, Ed, xiii, 157
palate, 22, 175
partials, 25, 54, 177
piano accompaniment, 28, 105, 109, 117,
    189, 196–98
pitch, 7, 11–12, 21–23, 25–31, 35–37,
    39, 40, 44, 48, 50, 54, 62, 65, 70, 84,
    90–92, 98–99, 118, 121, 138, 140, 142,
    156, 164, 174, 175, 178–79, 185
posture, 101, 107, 115, 194
practice journal, 63, 111–12
practice partner, 37, 84, 85, 117

Rachmaninoff, 154
Ravel, 94, 154–55, 158
recording, 56, 86, 87, 99, 101, 107, 109,
    116–18, 155, 160–61, 165, 170–72,
    191
reed clipper, 130, 146
reed rush, 127–29, 131–34, 146
reeds, 23, 39, 58, 64, 114, 119, 124–26,
    128, 130, 132, 135, 138, 146, 151–52,
    155, 158–59, 166, 168, 188, 195, 201
Reger, 168
register key, 69, 71, 80, 165
register tube, 25, 36, 144, 165
repertoire, 8, 20, 26, 56, 58, 64, 88, 95, 99,
    107, 111–12, 121, 153, 158, 162–63,
    166, 168, 172, 196

Rhapsody in Blue, 169, 179
Rigotti, 130
Rimsky-Korsakov, 154
rock, 171, 189
Romanian, 171, 173
Rossini, 3, 5, 113

Shaw, 169
Shostakovich, 154–55
sight-reading, 84, 88–90, 162, 189
singing, 21, 40, 59, 88, 90, 107, 174, 185,
    191
single tonguing, 19
slap tongue, 22–23
SmartMusic, 37, 105, 109, 117, 189
Smetana, 93, 154
soft reed, 39, 58, 121, 130, 173
Spring, Robert, xiii, 99, 198
staccato, 2, 3, 5–10, 12–13, 15, 17, 19–20,
    85, 113, 122
stage fright, 187
Strauss, 94, 154–55, 158, 195
Stravinsky, 89, 154–55
string players, 25, 62
swab, 36, 119, 144–45, 147–48, 151–52
synthetic reed, 23, 135, 146

Tchaikovsky, 154
technical independence, 89, 95
technology, 135, 189, 191
teeth, 11, 32–34, 59, 65, 98, 99, 122–23,
    149–50
tension, 10, 12–13, 33, 41, 44, 59, 73–74,
    76, 82, 101, 122
The Bartered Bride, 11, 70
throat b♭, 10, 25, 72, 140
thumb, 1, 65, 71–72, 78, 123–24, 136–37,
    142, 146, 151–52
t one, 9, 12–13, 15, 19, 21, 23, 25–27, 29–
    37, 39, 41, 43, 45, 48, 50, 52–58, 60–
    66, 68, 70–71, 80, 97, 102, 104, 108–9,
    111, 117–18, 121, 135, 149, 153, 166,
    179, 182–83, 185, 187, 189, 193

About the Author

Michele Gingras is Distinguished Professor Emerita of clarinet at Miami University (OH), where she was named Crossen Hays Curry Distinguished Educator and Distinguished Scholar of the graduate faculty. She performed and taught master classes worldwide, released more than a dozen CDs, and wrote two hundred articles and reviews for numerous international publications. She performed with the Cincinnati Klezmer Project for twenty years and concertizes with Duo2go and Miami3 throughout the United States. Gingras is past secretary of the International Clarinet Association and is an Artist Clinician for Buffet Crampon and Légère Reeds. She earned a *premier prix* from the Quebec Music Conservatory in Montreal and an M.M. in clarinet performance at Northwestern University. In 2017 she became instructor of clarinet at Butler University in Indianapolis.

Lightning Source UK Ltd.
Milton Keynes UK
UKHW030624131218
333811UK00010B/537/P